PLAY TO
WIN

5 PRINCIPLES TO SUCCEED
— IN LIFE AND BUSINESS —

PAUL WHITE

Play to Win
5 Principles to Succeed in Life and Business

ISBN 978-1-7366861-0-2

Published by Paul White Enterprises

CONTENTS

Introduction

LOVE A GOOD before and after story. When I flip on the sports channel, I can't help but pull for the underdogs and hope against all odds they can pull out a win. If your team has a terrible record and shows up on the field to go against the grain of every statistic and prediction, sweeping their division and becoming state champs having worked their tails off to prove everyone wrong, it gives you hope, doesn't it? No one on the sidelines believed they could do it. In fact, there were probably people wagering their hard-earned money on the belief that the team was going nowhere fast. In that case, you could even say people were rooting for them to lose.

I don't know about you, but that's a story I can relate to.

When you look at me today, you might be inclined to think that my life has always been this financially stable or that I was always in a respected place of leadership. But in reality, what you're seeing is my own *after*.

Today, I'm blessed to be a leader in my industry, with accolades and sales revenues that bump up against the billion-dollar mark when you put them all together. I've created opportunities for success and built a career that set me apart in my field. I've led organizations to win awards like "Dealer of the Year" and "Most Profitable Dealership" and increased annual performance rankings by double-digits during an economic era that sent many other dealerships into a downward spiral that they couldn't stop. I've spearheaded teams with more than 700 staff members and served as a mentor for franchise owners and personnel across stores and state lines. As I worked in every department a dealership has to offer and with almost every single U.S. and foreign automotive brand, the people I've met have given me invaluable perspective. But for me, part of sharing this *after* you see today is telling you the story that was my *before* and offering you the same principles I used to get here.

My *Before*

Like most people, my childhood wasn't the crisp, sunny version depicted in movies and on television. The son of a white father and a black mother, I had no clear box to check on school surveys. Being biracial meant I didn't quite fit into any community that was defined by a skin tone. My black classmates with a darker skin tone didn't see me as fully one of their own. But I wasn't exactly white either. Since neither group wanted to claim me, I learned at a young age that I would have to find ways to fill myself up. If I was going to learn something, I would have to do it on my own. There would be no built-in community for me to fall back on.

This dynamic of inequality and feeling like I didn't belong anywhere was tough to deal with at school, but at home I worked alongside my family members. I have two half-brothers, sons from my dad's previous marriage, who are both white. The three of us worked for my dad growing up at The Big Lot, one of the first independent used car stores in Dallas. While my older, white half-brothers were already managers and salesmen, I was put to work detailing cars. If I wanted to know how to sell a car the right way, my dad would say, I better know how to clean one. After detailing each car, my dad would then examine my work by running a toothbrush between the cracks along the hood and the fender to check for wax. It's an image that fills my mind every morning when I reach for my toothbrush, even now. My heart will quicken and my blood begins pumping harder, as my emotional muscle memory presses me to prepare for a day of wins.

On payday, the disparity between my older brothers and me was obvious. I can see now that I was younger and still learning the ropes, so I was paid what the work was worth. But when you're young and expecting rejection, your paycheck can feel like a statement of *your* worth.

As I've aged, I can see now how deeply affected I have been by those early family relationships. My dad was a veteran of World War II, and his military experience led him to parent with a firm hand. We boys were his soldiers, and he was determined to challenge us and teach us how to figure things out on our own.

My dad taught me that if I didn't know how to fix a problem or couldn't due to my own human fragility, I had better figure it out quick if I wanted to survive in this world. Toughness was his gospel.

This became all too real for me when I was five and my dad threw me into the deep end of a pool. Standing on the side of the pool, he told me I needed to learn how to swim or drown. Of course, he pulled me out when he realized that I was, in fact, going to drown.

Although he was a "pull yourself up by your own bootstraps" kind of guy who could be difficult to please, at a young age, I discovered that I could impress him with my skills as an athlete. I wasn't just athletic. I was faster than all the other kids in school and, as a kindergartener, I could throw a ball with the accuracy and power that would rival the abilities of some middle school boys. I leaned into this hard, as it was a reliable way for me to connect with my father and make him proud. So, at a school Field Day event at the age of seven, I beamed when I saw him appear beside me to watch me compete.

During the passing competition, I grabbed the baseball and prepared to throw one of my game-winning fastballs when, for a reason I'll never understand, the ball inexplicably fell out of my hand. It wouldn't have been a big deal for most seven-year-olds. But it was a crushing blow as I watched my father's face change from interest to disappointment. From that day on, I was fueled by a passion to one-up any competition that reared its head and climb higher and higher in the ranks of success.

Toughness at all costs may not have been my gospel, but winning came close.

As a teenager, that inescapable drive and motivation showed up on the football field. If my dad said two touchdowns before the half would make him proud, I scored four. I ascribed to my Mohamed Ali's saying: "Champions aren't built in the ring. They're built at 5 o'clock in the morning when no one's around." I pushed and pushed, training and preparing on my own, so that whenever a game day rolled around, I was ready. I didn't want to risk the possibility of not getting put in the game when there was a chance my dad might potentially be sitting in the stadium bleachers.

My parents eventually divorced when I was 13. With their broken ties, I was faced with an impossible choice: choosing to live with my mother and my black family or my father and my white family.

I was staying with my grandmother on my mother's side in the wake of their separation when one evening, as I was playing in the front yard, my dad pulled into the drive, declaring that he was moving to Las Vegas. He asked whether or not I wanted to come along too. Standing on that front lawn, I knew I wanted to be with him, even though it broke my heart to leave my mom. The phone call from Las Vegas, explaining to her for the first time that I had moved away and her tear-filled response is a moment I will never forget. No amount of toughness or wins can shield you from the immense pain that comes from hurting the people you love most. But I made the choice I thought was right for me at the time.

For better or worse, those youthful experiences changed me. I believe I am where I am today in part because of those early pressures to perform and excel. I felt a drive to work harder and be better than the older brothers I compared myself to, and I was constantly trying to outrun them and earn the smile and attaboy my dad would dole out when I achieved something remarkable. Though I wouldn't wish that kind of pressure on any young person, I can look back know and see the good that came out of those challenging times.

> **I can look back know and see the good that came out of those challenging times.**

By the age of 19, I branched out on my own and tried my hand at selling cars for someone other than my father. It was then I started a long professional path that has resulted in the principles you'll find in this book. That 19-year-old boy—scared, determined, and even a little angry—pushed hard to forge his own identity.

I had been conditioned to push and innovate. An impulse deep inside me propelled me ahead, even when things were tough. I believe that's why I didn't give up when my situation required me to start over and claw my way back through the trenches to get my life and financial stability back. And I believe that's why, when life was at its bleakest, I never gave up. I have always played to win.

Your *Before*

Maybe you've shied away from your *before* because it's messy, embarrassing, or just plain exhausting. If you're like me, your *before* is rough and even dark at times. This mess is our history and it can't be wrapped up in under 60 minutes like those mesmerizing transformations we see on ESPN. There's no camera crew to edit the rough spots down to a quick montage of old photos.

For those of us with a past we'd sometimes rather forget, we might be tempted to look around at the shiny *afters* belonging to others and wonder if our story could ever measure up, let alone compete. When all we see are the accolades and the finish line and the trophies hoisted over the winner's shoulders, it can seem as though the grueling training and recovery process that was required for those confetti-covered moments didn't exist.

When that feeling of hopelessness arises, I want to encourage you to see the value in your *before*. Those moments of victory we all love to applaud are only possible because someone decided to ignore their *before* status and push for the *after*. Those championship wins and top-selling products and record-breaking sales moments are possible because there were plenty of behind-the-scenes hours spent preparing for the big game, numerous years spent plugging away on a dream that no one believed in except the dreamer.

When your *before* status begins to feel like a chronic diagnosis that's got you trapped, remember that the biggest difference between winners and losers is whether or not they gave up. Even if someone is born with the financial means to go to an exclusive school or has the right connections, they still have to put themselves out there and take the risks that make them uncomfortable. We're all required to make sacrifices and work when the results aren't necessarily immediate in order to reach the elite level of our potential.

Whether you have every resource available to you or, like me, took off from a different starting line, it's time to own your *before* status. Mentally flip through the pages of your story and underline the parts that make you cringe. Grab a pen and paper, and go over what has shaped you into who you are today—not just the highlight reel and greatest moments, but the crushing mistakes, errors in judgment, and wounds that you've endured. Make a list. Write it out. Let it stare back at you. Now, on the roadmap of your life, realize that those challenging roadblocks and obstacles are simply part of the preparation for your journey—not the entire trip. They are the pit stops that remind you where the highway is, but not a place to camp out.

To keep myself on track, I like to visualize my entire life like a roadmap. There are endless twists and turns and possibilities around every corner. The turns that I make each day can either build up my life in ways that wouldn't be possible without the risks required by those unexpected detours. Or I could choose to ignore the opportunities, stick with what's familiar even if it's the wrong road, or worse, stop paying attention and just go where the road takes me.

I truly believe there is power in the everyday choices we make that often seem miniscule or safe. To finish out my day with a win, I need to stay accountable for every moment that day held. To get where I'm going on the roadmap of my life, I need to have a plan, a charted course, and a destination in mind, with every year and even every day accounted for. Without this driving and guiding force, I could potentially end up at any number of places. I don't plan a vacation with my family, load our suitcases in the trunk, gather everyone in the car, and then drive aimlessly for hours. That's not a vacation. That's an accident (or family meltdown) waiting to happen. When we plan to go nowhere, we often get there.

> **When we plan to go nowhere, we often get there.**

Instead, when I go on a trip, I want to drive so that I get to my targeted destination as quickly and efficiently as possible. It's alright to take the scenic route as long as you're alright with it taking twice as long to arrive. So too with life.

Most of us don't start out wanting live aimlessly, making money or working long hours with no goal in mind. We don't want to stick with a rhythm and routine simply because it's the way it's always been done. We don't want to use up our finite amount of time on a project that takes us away from our family only to discover that it led us nowhere fast. And we certainly don't want to work twice as long for half the payout simply because we're too afraid to try a different path or speak up for what we know we're worth.

When I hear an employee or colleague say they've chosen the play they're running because that's the way that a particular task has always been done, I stop them right there because that's the most expensive answer anyone could give.

Whether you're an executive or an entrepreneur, you always have to be searching for ways to sharpen your saw, to improve your business, and to deepen your relationships with your people. That's what this book will help you do. The price of failing to improve yourself is the failure of the people you're leading—not just your own. If you don't clear the path, you're just clogging the drains for the people below you who aspire to do more. It's not fair to you, and it's not fair to anyone who's looking to you for guidance when you refuse to innovate or lead in the way you know you should be doing.

If we settle for sticking to a routine simply for the sake of tradition, then we're not the right leader in the chair and we're absolutely stunting everyone's growth beneath us. If the leader at the front of the line doesn't continue to grow, then no one else on the team who follows in those footsteps will either.

Instead, let's explore ways that you can live your life with purpose. Let's begin with a destination in mind and a specific charted path that will allow you to get there, while maintaining a willingness to divert to a better or faster route if one becomes available.

In this book, I've assembled the understanding I've gained from long workdays, big wins, and countless fumbles I've made along the way. My hope is that you'll use these hard-earned teachings as encouragement and guidance for your own life, and that you'll pick up this book and use it as a map that can be applied to your own journey to your unique destination. I pray that it will inspire and guide you when the next turn doesn't seem obvious.

The Principles to Win

To make it easy to digest and simple to remember, I've condensed a lifetime worth of living and learning into five concrete principles. These principles are important because they'll help you construct your own roadmap and discern which way would be the healthiest, safest, and fastest path to your goals, while nurturing the relationships in your life as you grow and improve.

I've seen colleagues skyrocket in their careers, receiving accolades and high-fives from those they share a work life with, only to watch as their families fell apart in the process. They may have achieved success, but it was through endless hours at the office and at the expense of their homelife.

> ### *Winning at work and failing at home isn't a true win.*

Winning at work and failing at home isn't a true win. If you opened this booking thinking I'm going to provide you a step-by-step guide for how to win at all costs, then you came to the wrong place. Some prices are not worth paying, no matter what reward waits at the end of that road. My hope for you is that you'll be able to learn from the five principles in this book to create a system that you can use to win at both your career and your relationships.

I've adopted these five principles in my own life, and I believe they have the power to change every aspect of your journey for the better. We'll cover the principles together one chapter at a time so that you'll be able to really soak up their power and internalize their benefits.

First, we'll learn how to get our heads in the game by evaluating our mindsets. I'm always surprised at how few people really believe they have what it takes to win. If we don't believe in ourselves, why would anyone else? We'll do the mental work to discover if we truly believe we can win, and, if not, uncover the roots behind the driving belief we've adopted that we don't measure up.

We'll learn to use our home court advantage and surround ourselves with the right people in chapter two and learn from masters in crafts inside and outside of the automotive market who agree that you can't win on your own.

Then in chapter three, we'll discover how to be relentless in our pursuit and fuel our deep-down burning desires. Even if you were taught it's not nice to be relentless, you can develop the perseverance and drive you need to win.

In chapter four, we'll examine our expectations and learn to adjust them and our actions to suit our environment. When we're driven to win at all costs, we can make the fatal error of forgetting to look up and see the strides that others around us are making. By learning to take the temperature of the customer and market climate, we can make small adjustments that can prevent giant blunders in the long run.

Then as you discover how to succeed–and you will!–we'll learn why believing and acting on our belief that there is something bigger than ourselves in the world will keep us firmly planted on the right path.

One of my missions in life has to be a leadership coach for those who come after me. I want my life to be a vessel to help others become the best versions of themselves. Sharing my life lessons in this book, along with the twists and turns that took me down roads that led to success or ill-chosen paths that became dead ends, thrills me because I know the massive difference these principles can make in your life.

I'm no different than you are or anyone else doing their best to live a life of purpose. We all have the same potential to thrive, succeed, and win when we work with the right tools.

These principles have not only changed my life, they've saved my life from heading in the wrong direction or giving up whenever the opportunity presented itself. They have raised my potential and transformed my life. I know they can do the same for you. If you'll embrace these principles alongside me, internalize them, and make them your own, they will quickly become a part of your values and, ultimately, a part of you. I hope as you turn the pages with me, that you'll recognize the importance of building a roadmap and staying the course.

If you feel like you're too far behind the pack to catch up now or that you camped out too long at the starting gate and missed your chance to take off, I want to remind you that you still have what it takes. Picking up this book, which I believe will help you learn how to take off at full speed, proves that you are still in the race. You may be way off course, or your destination may

> **I wrote this book because I'm rooting for you.**

feel like it's lightyears away. But I encourage you to remember that, like the underdogs we love to root for, the most impressive *afters* often come in the wake of the most dismal of starts.

There's a reason why people love a Cinderella story. When everyone expects you to lose, it makes winning that much sweeter. Maybe you can relate to that feeling. You may be looking back over your career or your personal history, and "underdog" feels like a fitting title. You not only know what it feels like when everyone is expecting you to fail, you live with it every day. If so, I want you to know that I wrote this book because I'm rooting for you. In fact, my bet is on you.

It's time to learn how to transform a losing record into a winning one. It's time to take your wins and make them into the standard and not the exception. Turn the page, and let's go together.

CHAPTER 1

Get Your Head in the Game

MOST OF MY summers throughout childhood were spent in Ennis, Texas, with my grandmother. She never had much, as far as material possessions. She never even had running water. As a maid, the most money she probably ever made was on the third of every month when she was paid $300. Regardless of the conditions, I loved being around my grandmother.

During those hot and sticky Texas summers, with no indoor shower or sink to wash up in, I began to dream what I could become. I knew that these difficult conditions, albeit with the grandmother I adored, were not meant to be my forever situation. I began to focus on small accomplishments, wins I could claim and build upon, and then not letting anyone deter me from what I believed was mine for the taking, despite my family's lack of resources to give me a boost. I began to visualize my future.

World-record swimmer Katie Ledecky and the most decorated U.S. Olympian in history Michael Phelps do it. Tennis star Billie Jean King relied on it in the 1960s. Even Oprah Winfrey credits it as one of the reasons she landed her role in the movie *The Color Purple*.

It's not science fiction or new age fantasy. Visualization is a proven training method. Beyond dogged practice schedules and commitment to goals, this practice can make the difference between winners and those who work hard but ultimately fail to reach their destinations.

Your ability to make the right choices, follow the correct path, and be resourceful in the face of adversity are all amped up and reinforced by proper mental training. What are you doing to prepare your mind to win?

Too often, people want to skip this essential foundation of winning. They want to go right into the systems, processes, and strategies. They think if they just work the situation right, they'll come out on top. But if you go into a game without your head in the right place, you're much less likely to be on the winning side.

Just as an Olympian wouldn't skip a training day at the gym, so too anyone who wants to win won't skimp on preparing their mindset for the big leaps, risks, and obstacles ahead. Imagining yourself wading through all of those distractions and complications and then nailing it, in spite of whatever life throws at you, has become the not-so-secret weapon of high achievers in every walk of life.

The U.S. Olympics committee believes the value of visualization and mental preparation is so key to winning that they brought nine sports psychologists with them to the Sochi Olympics. And they aren't the only ones. The Canadian team brought eight sports psychologists, and the Norwegians brought three.

"People are recognizing that training the mind is just as important if not more important than training the body," sports psychologist Nicole Detling told the *New York Times* during their coverage of the Sochi Winter Olympics. "Mental skills are basically there to help you pull out your best performance when that best performance is necessary."

This visualization technique is not a casual pregame warmup. Olympic athletes have seen the benefits of visualization and now rely on it so much, they consider it a vital part of their training process. "I don't think I could possibly do a jump or especially a new trick without having this imagery process first," Emily Cook, a member of the U.S. freestyle ski Olympics team told the *New York Times*. "For me, this is so very key to the athlete that I've become."

GET YOUR HEAD IN THE GAME

What a Winning Mindset Actually Does for You

If you're thinking this all sounds like a lot of conjecture and not much hard evidence that you'd get similar results, consider a scientific study that *Business Insider* reported after the 2014 Olympics. Using Olympic athletes as the subjects, scientists studied and compared the training schedules of four groups of athletes:

- one group that spent 100 percent of their training focusing on their physical abilities
- a second group that focused 75 percent on physical training and 25 percent on mental training
- a third group that split the difference, spending equal time on both physical and mental training
- and a fourth group that spent only 25 percent of their training focused on the physical and 75 percent of their time focused on their mental training.

The results of the study showed that the fourth group, the ones who spent the majority of their time visualizing succeeding, were more likely to win. Those who pictured themselves crossing the finish line first actually did, even more so than their competitors who had dedicated hours and hours of their lives to transforming their bodies into athletic, performance machines.

So let me ask: Do you have a winning mindset? Maybe your immediate response has always been, "Of course, I do! Everyone wants to win!" But there is a vast difference between wanting to win and actually winning. Between wanting and getting what you want comes the preparation, mental tenacity, and grit to keep moving even when life feels like it has you glued to the floor.

Take an inventory of how you mentally approach your life, your goals, and the hindrances that you encounter on a day-to-day basis. Do you believe in possibility?

One of the first steps to winning is believing that you can. Often, the moment we feel that our dreams or goals are possible, it lasts only a flicker of time before our shame or our fear of failure shuts it down. When that happens, we feel like we're not only guarding ourselves from disappointment, we're also protecting those around us from the risks of what might happen if we flop.

> **One of the first steps to winning is believing that you can.**

In those moments it's important to realize that this kind of shame isn't honorable. It isn't what righteous people do. This type of shame zaps us of our power and ties our hands to prevent us from trying. We think we're caring for ourselves and others when what we're actually doing is throwing a gigantic pity party that keeps us from having to put ourselves out there. We may say we're trying to protect others, when we're really just thinking about ourselves.

But what if we automatically believed in our own abilities? What if we stopped pretending we were trying to help others by playing it safe and chose to go the dangerous route of believing we can? What if our gut response to a new idea or an exciting adventure was "That could work out great!"

Instead of assuming the worst or engaging with the fears that haunt you, imagine what could be possible if you would only say yes to yourself.

That self-confidence was essential when I started the first job I had outside of working for my dad when I was 19. I felt a lot of pressure the first time I walked through those doors to sell cars at a Dodge dealership in East Dallas. It was the first time I had to wear a necktie to work and for those early days I would walk in with a jumble of a cheap fabric necktie under my chin because I didn't know how to tie one. It was all new and entirely uncomfortable to me.

Even though my dad had always had high expectations of me, these expectations were different – no matter how mad he might get if I didn't pass muster, I knew I had a place at his lot. But the sales process at car dealerships in those days was so cutthroat that the understanding was perform or hit the road. My livelihood was on the line every day I walked through the door.

Sales was not a cooperative environment. We each knew what was at stake if someone else scooped up the majority of the sales each month because on a whiteboard in the manager's office was a list of all our names and corresponding sales. At the end of the month, the General Manager would write our names and sales numbers out in rank order—from most cars sold to least—and the salesperson whose name appeared on the bottom row knew he was out. There didn't even need

> *...imagine what could be possible if you would only say yes to yourself.*

to be a conversation or an awkward firing experience. Everyone knew there was an unspoken rule: The last one on the board is the first one out the door. That was pretty motivating, as you can imagine.

At 19, I didn't have the same experience and maturity, or the secure and healthy family foundation that many of the other guys on the sales floor had. Heck, I couldn't even tie my own necktie before I came to work on the first few days. But every morning when I walked through those doors, I would visualize myself as a leader and as a salesman who made things happen. I would picture my day, the cars on the showroom floor and the customers that stepped onto the parking lot, and I would watch myself sell cars, one by one. At the end, I would wrap up my thoughts with the image of that daunting whiteboard rectangle. I would see the stack of names and I would envision their placement, making sure to never view my name as the one scribbled in marker at the bottom of that leaderboard. I'm proud to say that I never had a sales month at that store when I looked up to see my name in the hotseat, and I never experienced that sad walk of shame that accompanied anyone who realized they hadn't measured up to the coworkers who became their competition.

Tap the Power of Words

Believing in yourself and seeing yourself is just one step forward toward your goals. I believe there is power in our words—whether we speak them or write them—that can alter our futures when we are willing to internalize and act on what we say and write.

Actor Jim Carrey is one of the most well-known examples of someone who believed in himself and his talent and then used visualization and words as tools to reach his goals. Prior to his mega blockbuster hits like *Liar Liar, The Truman Show,* and *Ace Ventura: Pet Detective,* Carrey was a broke actor with big dreams of making millions and working with respected giants in his field.

During those lean years in the '80s , he would drive down to Mulholland Drive and park every night. There, he would visualize himself working with directors he admired and imagine people he looked up to saying things like, "I admire your work." It was almost a type of anesthetic for him, helping him deal with the anxiety that comes with the territory of being a low-paid actor with big dreams but no prospects on the horizon.

Believing was a way to get through those disheartening times, but he took it one step further in an effort to prove to himself that he was worthy. With no guarantee of any high-paid work in the future, he wrote himself a check for $10 million and post-dated it by a few years. He folded the check into his wallet, and over the next few years, watched it deteriorate and fade. Just as the date the check was written approached, he booked a gig for a movie titled Dumb and Dumber. His salary for that movie? Ten million dollars.

Believing in yourself and speaking or writing it into being gives you an advantage, a head start on everyone else standing at the starting gate. Now, writing a check and sticking it into your wallet isn't going to manifest a few million into your bank account. Even Carrey says he worked hard for his dreams and kept pushing in the direction of his goals. Just picturing your dreams won't make them happen. Or, as Carrey is famously quoted: "You can't just visualize and then go eat a sandwich." Working hard is an essential part of the equation, but working hard without the belief and the verbal proof that you believe in yourself and your dreams is going to make the road that much more difficult.

> *Believing in yourself and speaking or writing it into being gives you an advantage, a head start on everyone else standing at the starting gate.*

To get the most bang for your effort, I recommend a three-pronged approach that starts with believing you can. Think through the steps it takes to reach your goal, win the race, make the perfect sales pitch, or nail a public speaking presentation. What would it take to become the highest earning salesperson on your team or the leader that everyone comes to for wisdom? Imagine yourself taking the actions that will lead you to those opportunities and then picture yourself winning. Envision yourself at the top of your industry or cashing a six-figure paycheck or buying a home for your family. See yourself succeeding.

You've heard put your money where your mouth is. I'd like to propose you put your mouth where your mind is. Meaning, whatever your dreams are, say them out loud. Tell your partner or friend. Repeat them in the shower when no one but you is listening. It's not who you tell, but what you tell.

Then make your aspirations even more real by putting pen to paper. Write them down on a stickie note and put it on your bathroom mirror or the corner of your computer screen at work so that you'll be reminded every single day that you're working toward something real. Grab a spiral notebook and journal your dreams, even if it's just a one-page sheet of bullet points, so that the things you want in life are tangible and visible to you on a daily basis. Or maybe, like Carrey, you need to write yourself a hefty paycheck and then put yourself to work to make it a reality.

The part that stops many of us before we start is planning. This is where the dream becomes the to-do list, and it's typically the part many of us shy away from. Stop for a moment and think through how you're going to make your dreams come true. Do you need more education or a specific certification? Who could teach you how to get from where you are right now to where you want to go? Do you need a business plan or an investor? What is the one thing you could do today that will bring you an inch closer to the finish line tomorrow?

This is not about setting up a stack of unattainable leaps you have to complete marathon-style for six months. Instead, make a plan by choosing intentional baby steps that will lead you where you want to be at a sustainable rate. What's the next baby step you can take?

As you imagine what you want in life, believe you deserve the opportunity and then begin to take action steps toward those goals. Opportunities will probably arrive sooner than you expected. Life rewards those who show up, so don't be surprised when the next rung on the ladder toward your success reveals itself to you. And, I have to warn you, this is when these big dreams and seemingly faraway goals might seem a little scary. Because they start to get real.

The fun adventures that sounded good on paper—traveling around the world sharing a message that means something to you, training with people who are further along the path than you, accepting a new position or transferring to a new department, agreeing to give a presentation to a crowded room—these steps toward your goals are exciting but they can also be daunting! I want to encourage you to say yes to these chances that present themselves to you. Even when you think you're not ready. Even when you aren't sure you'll get it right. Say yes.

Say yes because opportunities are abundant but not often redundant. Be encouraged that there is an infinite stream of opportunity for you. If you miss the boat, it doesn't mean you'll be on the dock forever. But I do want to stress to you that if you say no to a specific opportunity once, it is likely that that same opening or break will not offer itself to you again. And worse, the next one may be slow in pulling into shore. Opportunity and luck favor those who show up. If you are physically or financially able, show up.

> Say yes because opportunities are abundant but not often redundant.

I believe in this approach because I have seen the benefits of it taking shape in my own life. As I progressed through my career in the automotive industry, I took each next step as it came. I poured myself into every department of every store location where I was stationed and said yes to the right opportunities as they came my way. That meant watching and learning from the older salespeople at that first dealership in East Dallas to learn the tactics of success. It meant showing up earlier than everyone else and staying later, saying yes to bold actions, like moving to North Carolina where I worked sunup to sundown and became the general manager of a dealership and then moving back to Texas where my career really took off.

Creating a Vision for Others

When I was 32, I was offered one of the most pivotal opportunities of my career. I was working for a national organization when a general manager at one of the Dallas locations retired. The organization began a national search for a world class operator to replace him. In the interim, I was asked to hold down the fort. But I didn't just sit in another man's chair. I went to work making things happen. So after four months of serving as interim manager, and at the age of 32, I became the youngest partner in an auto group of 60-plus dealerships.

Today, I'm one of the people who has the privilege and honor of doling out those opportunities I craved in my younger years. And I can tell you with absolute certainty who I love to give them to: people who believe they are the ones for the job, who show up and engage with their roles, and who take the action steps necessary to make their positions the most efficient, effective, and productive they can be.

One of my favorite success stories that I've had the honor of playing a role in is that of my Assistant Finance Director who was promoted to my store from a location in Wichita Falls. She was reliable and hardworking, and after just a few weeks, she approached me about her future at the company. She was looking to buy a townhome in the area but wanted confirmation from me that I envisioned her as part of the company and that specific location in the years to come before she put money down on a long-term investment.

She was putting her belief in herself into words by speaking up and asking for what she wanted. Then she put action behind her words by giving her work all that she had. Having witnessed her drive and the manner in which she showed up for work—on time and on mission—I was happy to tell her to go ahead with her investment. Soon after, I promoted her because I could see that she was doing her own job and the job her boss should have been doing. Today, with her work ethic and belief in herself, she is one of the most successful general managers in Houston. With her tenacity and belief system, she went from earning $75,000 a year as an assistant finance director, to earning over three-quarters of a million dollars—and that's on a bad year.

When you envision your own success, you can mentor those coming up behind you to do the same. But if you don't take responsibility for the direction you're going, you're not going to be the kind of leader your people need. You can't inspire others if they don't aspire to be where you are. That means you've got to practice visualizing your future, your goals, and your mentorship to others. You've got to hold a vision for them too—sometimes before they can hold one for themselves.

When Your Vision Is Clouded

You know now that getting your mind right is perhaps more important than the actionable steps you plan and then execute to reach your goals. But that mental preparation can be a double-edged sword for those who don't wield it correctly.

I've found that some people, because of their upbringing or shortcomings in the past, find it difficult (if not impossible) to see themselves winning even on the virtual playing field. This is especially true for people who grew up in poverty or in the projects. Our relationships with our parents, our circle of influence, and many other undercurrents influence how we think. It's going to be difficult for someone living in the projects to visualize victory. They have to find a place that they can't see with their eyes, but rather with their mind. If you can create that victorious vision in your mind, it can develop the right mindset that allows us to go places mentally that we've never even experienced or seen firsthand. We have to have that deep down inside of us, otherwise everything else around us will try to convince us that it's not possible.

Most of us would like to think of ourselves as winners, but when it comes down to it, too often the fear that we won't measure up invades our psychological truth, which can, in turn, become our actual truth. I want you to become brutally honest with yourself about your relationship with adversity and failure. Is it what you expect of yourself? Has life dealt you a hand so tough that you just assume it will always be this way? Do you picture yourself failing?

Or maybe you have someone on your team who sees themselves in this limited way. While you cannot step into their shoes and know exactly how they're feeling or what they're thinking, you can reach out in empathy to show them that your road hasn't always been easy either. You can encourage them to envision something greater for themselves by setting a time aside to walk with them through their ideal future, career, and relationships. This extra work with your team members can mean the difference between their success and failure—and by extension the success and failure of your organization.

American Olympian Jacqueline Hernandez can relate to those overwhelming feelings we all have at times. A competitor in the Olympic snowboard cross, she was left reeling after a traumatic crash that left her with significant injuries to the bone and nerves in her arm. An incredible athlete, she put in the hours and hours of grueling recovery and rehabilitation required to come back to the sport for the next Olympics. But as she recovered, she battled fears that she would again crash and suffer similar or worse injuries. Even in her visualization preparatory work, she fought against negative thoughts and the image of herself once again crashing. She would try to visualize herself crossing the finish line first but couldn't stop herself from leaning into the anxiety and possibility that she might crash again and injure herself or worse. Her fears were very real to her. After all, it wasn't whether a devastating crash could happen—it already had!

When she left the starting line on her next Olympic run, the uncertainties and anxiety she battled in her visualization came true, leading her to crash in her first run and incur a concussion and loss of consciousness before she was transported down the mountain by emergency personnel for medical attention.

Some people may look at that failure and tie it to bad luck. Maybe you think nothing can stop a failure from happening if a person is just unlucky. I hear people all the time say, "She just can't catch a lucky break," or "what an unlucky turn of events." Even people who ascribe wholeheartedly to the idea of luck know it doesn't make any sense to chalk every disappointment in life up to chance, but we do it so skillfully and subtly we often don't even notice we're doing it.

Not getting picked for a promotion we were hoping for is a drastically different circumstance than not having your raffle ticket drawn out of a hat, but I can't count the number of times I have heard someone say in an office environment, "I'm just not very lucky." When I hear those words, it makes me cringe, not only because I believe that luck isn't the driving factor in our successes and failures, but also because I know that what we say about ourselves matters and what we say about others matters.

We speak so much negativity into our own lives, that when it actually happens we're not surprised. When we chalk our missed opportunities up to bad luck, what we're really doing is proudly telling ourselves, "I told you so." We prefer proving ourselves right to winning, even if it means missing out on a life-changing opportunity. What a tragedy that we expect ourselves to blow it before we even get a chance to take off!

It's easier to blame our missteps on dumb luck because the fear of failure is real, and it can be debilitating. Fear is what keeps us from going on the trip of a lifetime because we hate flying, or not asking someone out because we can't bear the risk of embarrassment if the other person says no. We are well acquainted with fear, especially the fear that comes right before a fall.

If you've ever tried to stay upright on skis or roller skates or a surf board for the first time, you know what this visceral sensation feels like. It's not a feeling that arrives in an inkling. It's more of a butterfly in the stomach, "this might be how I die" feeling. And it's almost impossible to do any of these activities for the first time without standing on knees that wobble like a toddler's and flapping your arms like a duck as you try to find the center of gravity and get your balance. In the midst of all of your best physical efforts, as you frantically flail and struggle to stay balanced, you intuitively blurt out:

"I'm going to fall!"

And most of the time, what happens?

You fall.

It's almost as if in that moment, we need ourselves to fall. We so strongly expect it will happen, that if we don't fall, we're shocked to still be vertical. We'll look around in surprise and ask our friends nearby, "Did you see me?! I can't believe I did it!"

If success surprises you, it's likely you won't be surprised often.

When we need ourselves to fail or fall, and then live out a self-fulfilling prophesy by doing so, we engage the parts of our belief systems and hearts that tell us we are not ready for the next chance that could be waiting around the corner. We don't return voicemails or emails that could lead to a new job or volunteer role because we're scared that we'll say the wrong thing or prove ourselves right by failing again. We don't enroll in a new class or join a new study group because we can't bear the thought that everyone else will see the uneducated fool we already know ourselves to be. When we've listened to the negative self-talk that we've drilled into our own minds for years or decades, showing up for anything remotely scary or unknown can feel

> *If success surprises you, it's likely you won't be surprised often.*

like a nightmare. So, we say no. We turn down offers. We stay hidden. We don't raise our hand. We don't show up for our own lives and ultimately don't show up for our futures.

Living every day with a winning mindset takes concerted, consistent effort. It's a daily choice to believe that you are worthy and capable and that good things can and will come your way. Living with a mindset that doesn't lead to winning is much easier.

Maybe you feel your brain has been pre-programmed to expect failure. It's the default mode for most of our minds. Not sure you're out of default mode? Test yourself. If you call out your own failures more than your wins, you aren't living with a winning mindset. If you experience minor pushback and immediately pull back and say, "I shouldn't have even tried,"

> *Living every day with a winning mindset takes concerted, consistent effort.*

you aren't living with a winning mindset. If you don't get the Christmas bonus you were hoping for or find yourself perpetually single, and chalk all of it up to a simple stroke of bad luck, you are not living with a winning mindset.

Just as powerful and positive visualization isn't the only thing that leads us to success (hard work is essential too) so also a negative mindset isn't the only thing that can drag you down. A negative mindset doesn't mean you'll always fail, but if your vision is clouded, winning will be exponentially more difficult. As automotive legend Cecil Van Tuyl said, "Whether you think you can, or you can't, you're right!"

Developing a winning mindset may not come naturally for you, but with practice you'll learn to not only expect wins but act like a win is on its way. Mastering visualization is not just for Olympic athletes. It's a key component for your progress in life and in business. You're not likely to swim or ski at the same level that an Olympic athlete does any time soon, but you will be a competitor—whether that's competing for a coveted spot in graduate school, edging out an opposing firm to gain a new client, or winning a bid for a new construction project. Practice waking through what you're about to do.

If you have an interview, picture yourself walking through the front doors of the building, riding the elevator to the top floor, and then sitting in the lobby near the receptionist's desk. Imagine your potential boss waving you into her office and gesturing you towards a chair across from her desk. Go through the interview process meticulously, answering questions and preparing for distractions, and then picture yourself shaking her hand and hearing the words, "You're hired."

This process might feel slightly childish and imaginative the first few times you attempt it, but the effects and results are undeniable. Visualization doesn't guarantee you'll get the job, but it does make it more likely that you'll answer confidently and appear more prepared during the interview, which will undoubtedly increase the odds in your favor.

Les Brown says that once you find something that you truly want to do, you need to go after it, and the how and the why is none of your business. I believed in myself, even as a child at my grandmother's house during those hot Texas summers. I'm sure there's a time in your life when you can think back to your own determination to keep pushing forward, even when you had no idea how you were going to get from point A to point B. The key with this principle of visualization is to tap into that determination, hopefulness, and self-belief every day and use it as fuel to keep you going.

If you find that you're quick to penalize yourself for failure, it's likely that you decided on failure before it actually ever happened. Dig behind that action to unearth the thought lurking beneath it. Was a part of you expecting yourself to stumble? If so, I want to encourage you to give yourself more grace. Treat yourself the way you'd want a loved one to be treated. Pat yourself on the back for trying and make a plan right then and there that you'll try again soon. Whether you believe it yet or not, our world needs the unique brand of talent and strength that only you possess. So, pick yourself up and dust off your jeans, suit, or running shorts. We need you in the game.

— CHAPTER 2 —

Use Home Court Advantage

I T CAN BE difficult to remember that the people who we view as extremely successful were not necessarily born that way. They didn't wake up one morning with multiple books on the *New York Times* bestseller list or fill stadiums with thousands of fans out of nowhere. All of that success was preceded by a lengthy process of trial and error, of honing a craft, and, inevitably, a chorus of rejections and naysayers who thought their dream would never be well-received by readers, listeners, or buyers.

When we receive a rejection and hear the word "no," our automatic gut reaction is to receive that rejection as a personal insult. When our labor of love or idea or experience is deemed not viable by the gatekeepers or promoters in our specific industry, it can feel like an attack on our credibility and a hit to our self-esteem. The difference between people with really great ideas who get published or hired or who have investors flocking to their door and the people who have really great ideas but receive none of those things is their persistence, perseverance, and willingness to push past all the no's until they finally receive the yes they were hoping for.

Before Stephen King was *Stephen King* he was an aspiring writer who lived off the spontaneous paycheck he received from short stories published in men's magazines—mostly pornographic ones like *Playboy* and *Cavalier*. When King describes those early years of writing, it's as if the fire to write was coursing through his veins. Even when his writing was sporadically well-received and the jobs were not plentiful, he had a burning passion in his chest that made him feel like he was put on this planet to write. Unfortunately, publishers didn't agree. His first three manuscripts, which would eventually be published later and become the hits *Rage*, *The Long Walk*, and *Blaze*, were flatly rejected.

King continued to write for men's magazines, but readers began to criticize his short stories, saying they felt like King wrote too macho—that he wouldn't or couldn't write from a woman's perspective. Instead of sending him cowering in defeat, the criticism fueled him, and King began writing a short story about a young bullied high school girl whose surge of hormones as she begins menstruation gives her heightened telekinetic powers. His story idea would eventually become the book and movie we know today as *Carrie*.

But three pages in, realizing that his critics could be right and he might not have what it took to write literature with an authentic female lead after all, and discovering that the story couldn't be told in the short story format the magazines required, he crumpled the pages into balls and threw them in the wastepaper basket. When his wife, Tabitha, saw the papers peeking out of the laundry room trash the next day, she pulled them out, dusted them off, read them, and completely disagreed with King's dismissal of the work. He didn't believe in himself, but she did. With her help understanding the world of women and the environment inside of girls' high school locker rooms, King penned the novel in nine months and submitted it to thirty publishers. This is where we expect a wild success story. Instead, all thirty rejected him.

Now, it seemed, publishers were reinforcing the doubt he had felt so strongly that led him to trash the novel in the first place. Thirty publishing professionals and experts couldn't be wrong, could they? Maybe he didn't have what it took after all. He must have allowed himself to agree with the doubters, even if for only a moment.

His reservations vanished when the editor from Doubleday Publishing sent a telegram informing him that they had bought the book for $2,500. Even back then $2,500 wasn't a huge sum, but it was the beginning of a publishing empire, as *Carrie* sparked the flame in what would become a wildfire, making King the nineteenth bestselling author of all time.

If King hadn't had a Tabitha in his life, someone who would push back against the doubts and the more traditional routes he could have taken, and instead encourage him to continue to believe in his dreams, we wouldn't have the legendary novels only his brain could create, like *It* or *The Shining*. Can you imagine what the world would have missed out on if Stephen's wife hadn't dug those lint-covered pages out of the trash can? "Tabby always knew what I was supposed to be doing, and she believed that I would succeed at it," King said during his acceptance speech at the National Book Awards in 2003.

For King, one *yes* from Doubleday Publishing was all it took to establish a legendary career that would lead to more than 350 million books sold, support his family, and allow him to pursue his passion for writing full-time. But before that yes, was an affirmative role just as crucial that King found in his wife, Tabitha. Without her, the story could have had a much different ending. The Kings, according to Stephen, would likely still be living in a trailer or some other rundown housing settlement, and he would be standing in front of a whiteboard teaching English instead of tapping away in front of a keyboard, crafting legendary tales and doing what he loves most.

The Three Types of People on the Court

What Tabitha provided for Stephen is a home court advantage that all of us need if we're going to push past the naysayers and rejections that will be inevitable in our futures. I understand that this advantage doesn't come built in for all of us, but I want you to know that the family or social environment that came automatic for you is not your only option.

You may not immediately agree that you have a home court advantage, but everyone—for better or for worse—has a circle of influence filled with people who greatly impact how we think about ourselves and others. From our mothers and fathers and those who we allow to speak into our lives to those who we invite to be a part of our lives, the people we surround ourselves with influence how we think and how we approach our goals. There are a lot of undercurrents to this mindset, and it's very difficult to see it from the inside looking out. That's why I spend a lot of time with my team explaining the differences in the big three types of people I call Caretakers, Playmakers, and Game Changers.

Caretakers are baseliners. They covet the spotlight, but when they get put into those big moments, they can't handle it most of the time. They "puke under pressure," as I like to tell my teams. They're most comfortable in a "holding down the fort" mentality that keeps them somewhat consistent and makes them someone you can count on for the most part, but they never help things thrive. In my absence, Caretakers tend to focus on just keeping things afloat until I get back. I define integrity by doing the envelope-pushing things I would want them to be doing even when I'm not there to watch it happen. That means Caretakers and I don't tend to get along very well because I want my teams to invest in the business and help it grow, not just keep it running.

Playmakers are less common, but I do my best to surround myself with them. These are the people that push the process along thanks to their natural talent. They know how to utilize their specific talents to get results, and sometimes those results are stellar. But that can often be to their detriment because leaning on their remarkable talent alone allows them to take shortcuts in other areas. Playmakers keep the ball rolling and make profits accelerate, but their lazy dependence on their own natural talents keep them from being more well-rounded and becoming what we ultimately all should strive to become: Game Changers.

You can recognize a Game Changer best when an office environment spirals into panic mode. During those feverish moments, a Game Changer can remain calm and change the atmosphere around them into a functional and effective one with their leadership. Game Changers perform their best when the pressure is at its worst. Game Changers are high-level players who are focused on results and are committed to winning by setting an example

> **Game Changers perform their best when the pressure is at its worst.**

of going after their goals every single day. They are hyper-focused and exude a relentless spirit and attitude.

Game Changers are my go-to people. They're the ones who everyone calls when the team needs a surefire win. Michael Jordan is one of the most obvious and well-known Game Changers in sports history. He loved the spotlight, and in the toughest moments, he shone brightest as he leapt over competitors with his now famous spread-eagle dunking style.

Although controversy has swirled around him, I believe Tom Brady belongs in the ranks of Game Changer as well. Under his leadership, the New England Patriots have gone to the Super Bowl nine times, six of which he helped bring home a winning Super Bowl ring. Watching Tom Brady means accepting the fact that no game is over until the clock ticks down to zero. Brady has never lost a playoff game that went into overtime, and when the NFL rules changed to dictate that overtime was a sudden death match, his opponents often never got a chance to touch the ball. In post-game interviews, Brady's teammates have been quoted as saying that when a game goes into overtime, they're not worried about anything because they've seen how those games end. When the clock is ticking down and the stadium is one loud roar, Brady brings home a win—the epitome of a Game Changer.

When you look at sports giants like Michael Jordan and Tom Brady, there is an obvious elite level of talent that sets them apart. And yes, I believe their talent makes the difference for them in their specific roles, but I also know that their relentless drive and hyper-focused mindset make their wins consistent, not just possible.

Identifying the natural roles and working styles of the people around you is essential because there's only one you and you only have so many hours in a day. Another way of describing the different types of people I encounter in the workplace is drivers, drainers, and maintainers.

Applying the Home Court Advantage

The home court advantage is something you can receive—from people who believe in you like Stephen King's wife believed in him—and something you can give.

I work hard to offer my team the home court advantage, but as a leader with finite time and resources, it's my responsibility to identify where I can spend my time that will result in maximum reward. I have to spread my time like Miracle Whip®, making sure that I'm intentional and proactive about my choices.

I determine quickly whether a person deserves my time or not because my time and my talent are my greatest assets. I have to ensure that both of those get used every day to the best of my ability because I won't get either of them back. It's imperative that I'm pouring into the right person who has the bandwidth to absorb and apply what I'm offering. For the people who do have the energy and mindset to take in everything I'm trying to teach, I'm a hands-on teacher who walks side-by-side with them on a daily basis until they're able to level up their successes.

You need to be one of the people offering your team members the home court advantage. If they aren't getting encouraged, helped, and supported by you, you're missing an opportunity.

Of course, to offer help to others, you've got to be willing to receive it yourself.

To check your home court advantage, it's a good idea to give your social circle a checkup. If you determine that you don't have a home court advantage, you'll need to create one. We all know what it's like to stand around the water cooler and listen to the negativity and gossip that pervades office culture. Water cooler conversations have their place, but if those critical structures are your foundation for friendships, then it will be difficult to switch off that negativity when it comes time to perform or put yourself out there in the workplace in a vulnerable way. And I can attest to the fact that vulnerability and risk are vital for truly great achievements.

> *...to offer help to others, you've got to be willing to receive it yourself.*

When you step back and look at your circle of work friends, are all of them in the same situation as you or lower? The fastest, most effective way to improve your career is by watching and learning from someone who is already where you want to go. Who do you know that is living out the career you aspire to? If you can't name a single person in that role, then it's time to widen your friendship pool.

Mentors have long been lauded as the necessary key to winning on the professional level, but, if I'm honest, finding someone who is willing to give of themselves in that capacity can be extremely difficult to find. If finding a mentor seems improbable, tap into the hundreds, if not thousands, of gurus and experts available on YouTube or on podcasts or blogs in your specific industry and niche. Soak up their advice and action plans, and then follow what they suggest.

As a young man, I had the opportunity to work under Cecil Van Tuyl, the founder of a renown auto group, today part of one of the largest dealership groups in America. This man's strong mentorship provided me with the tools and confidence I desperately needed to climb as high as I have. But I recognize that not everyone has their own mentor in this way.

It's imperative that someone has belief in you until your own belief in yourself kicks in. In my career, my experience is that life does not come at you in gentle or subtle ebbs and flows or peaks and valleys, but in extreme mountain tops and treacherous canyons. I have had giant victories, like working my way up the ranks to eventually become the General Manager and youngest Partner ever at a dealership in Dallas, where I helped the organization reach record-setting annual revenue of $240 million and the largest volume gains and market share since its inception. I know that those accomplishments are in part because my mentor showed me how. But, as I alluded to earlier, I've also walked through the lowest of lows that I never imagined I'd recover from.

> *It's imperative that someone has belief in you until your own belief in yourself kicks in.*

Getting Through the Dark Days

After my revered mentor became ill and the ownership and management of his dealerships changed, I began looking for different opportunities. My friend, who at the time was coaching a professional sports team, was doing a tremendous amount of marketing with me. We were in TV commercials side-by-side and our faces were all over town on billboards. My friend decided he wanted to get into the car business, so we met with a gentleman I knew who had 18 stores at the time. After our meeting, we decided to go in together on our own store. I became Platform President over his group of stores, and we had some very successful months where I helped increase the annual performance by 15 percent and boost the expanded market share by 20 percent.

And then the recession of 2008 happened. The business we had acquired just didn't look the same any longer, and our plan for success turned into a plan for survival. My friend had an opportunity in professional sports that he felt was more lucrative and a better fit, so he ended up amicably leaving our team. In the wake of his absence, the other partners in the business who were majority owners, took the company in a direction that was in opposition to what I believed was the best course of action, and unfortunately, I turned out to be right.

It was the beginning of one of the lowest points in my career. I lost a tremendous amount of money. When people say the grass is greener, I always tell them to check the water bill. I had an enormously tall water bill at that time. We had been riding high, on the heels of my friend's celebrity status and our press buzz, but when the economic bubble hit, the game changed.

We were deep in debt and there was no profit to give us hope. The substantial amount of money that was owed to me through the business was put toward the deficit. I left the organization without a dime and driving a car that I didn't own.

My sales fleet and all of the cars I previously held the titles to had been sold to pay for the divorce. Between that and the business dissolution, I was left with nothing. It was a very dark moment for me.

> I went from being a guy who owned 40 cars to a guy who could barely hold onto one.

That darkness lingered for almost a year. My home in McKinney was several months behind payment, and even after the sale, there was no money left over for me. At the time I was a single father to my then-five-year-old son. We moved in with my girlfriend, and I felt depression come over me stronger than anything I've ever felt before in my life.

I went from being a guy who owned 40 cars to a guy who could barely hold onto one. How do you recover from making millions a year as a Partner, to becoming a guy who can't pay for groceries? I can't even describe how tough that time was for me.

I'll be vulnerable and admit that this dark year was one where I dangled on the edge of being suicidal. For a while, my faith kept me alive, but as things got tougher, even that wasn't enough to sustain me. The only reason I'm on this planet today is my son. I would look at him and know that I couldn't leave him. He kept me alive.

I knew I had to dig myself out of this hole, so I spent every day in a coffee shop bookstore that had a play area for kids and free internet, searching for a job online. My son would play, and I would work the phones, calling dealers and pretending that I had heard they were looking for someone with my experience.

While some people might criticize me and say I should have taken whatever job I could find, it was very important to me that the trajectory of my career was not compromised on paper, even though I was in a very desperate situation. I needed my new role to maintain my professional status and keep an upward trend if I was ever going to reach the heights that I knew I was meant to reach. I knew my talent had not diminished, but I was going to have to fight through these changes.

As I sought new work, my girlfriend would accompany me from coast to coast for interviews, helping with the driving burden. On one of our most memorable trips, we had $185 in our pocket for the entire journey. We were tired as could be one evening when we pulled into Arizona, and we knew we had to get a room and sleep before we could drive any further. We pulled up to the Ritz Carlton, and she parked and said, "I have a great idea. Let's sleep in the back of my car."

It was a gut punch for me to watch her sleeping in the car next to me and not have the funds to pay for a hotel room. But her belief in me was so strong that she was willing to go through this with me. I gave her my word right then and there that from that moment on, any hotel anywhere on the globe that she wanted to stay at, she could point her finger on a map and she would be able to stay there. I've since kept my word hundreds of times.

But in that moment, as she slept in the car, she couldn't have known for certain that I would keep my promise. Other who helped me along the way, opening their hearts and homes to me, couldn't have known for sure that I would be a man of my word down the line. Without their support, I would have floundered and probably even thrown in the towel. But others have been in my corner even though the odds were stacked against me and I had nothing to offer them at the time. Throughout that year and all the years since, they have been my home court advantage. They believed in me even when I didn't believe in myself. Because of that unwavering belief, I persisted until I finally landed the right job for me and the right next step in my career.

> They believed in me even when I didn't believe in myself.

What It Means to Be a Fan

As you hear my story, you might be able to pinpoint one person in your own life—or more than one, if you're especially blessed—who is there to encourage you when the path seems bleak. Think about the high value of what those people have to offer and how they have poured into your life when you felt dry and empty. The people who invest in your life when you're having the toughest of days are the relationships we need to intentionally lean into and gravitate toward.

Everyone loves to show up when the wine is flowing, the cars are new and shiny, and the money is stacked deep, but it's the people who continue to show up when everything has fallen apart, when you can't pick up the tab for everyone at the table, and when you don't have the energy to keep getting up and face another tough day who really keep us moving in the right direction.

Sometimes, our home court advantage is there for us even when we don't expect it. My dear friend, who I mentioned in the previous chapter had worked as my Assistant Finance Director, is one of those people. After I left that dealership in 2007 to branch out with my own store, this wonderful friend invited us to stay with her for a few months at her house. She fed us and made us feel welcome, and as I spent more time around her, I began to feel more and more inspired.

My friend reminded me of what times were like when I could take my finance team on weekend getaways, buy them gifts, or offer a helping hand when someone else needed it. She could remind me of all the incredible moments that I just didn't call to mind and remember on my own because of the deep pit of despair that had swallowed me.

With her encouragement and sense of homecoming, I felt my backbone straighten and strengthen. I called and confirmed that all of the corporate entities involved knew that the downfall of the dealership I had been a part of wasn't due to any lack of automotive acumen or horsepower on my part. As a result of that phone call, I got a tip about a gentleman in the New York and New Jersey market who had ten dealerships in all and was looking for a strong and experienced Vice President of Operations. They described him as a hardcore guy, and I knew, looking back at where I had come from, that I was tailor made for the role.

The people who invest in your life when you're having the toughest of days are the relationships we need to intentionally lean into and gravitate toward.

We drove to New York and I got the job. I can't even describe the out-of-body feeling I had in that moment. We went from having nothing to a job with a salary that would allow us to start over. Over the course of the previous nine months, as we had crisscrossed the country in search of a high-level automotive position for me, there were definitely times when it seemed like I would never recover, that there would be no quick turnaround or magical transformation.

My relief didn't arrive quickly, and the multimillion-dollar salary and lavish home with luxury cars parked in the driveway I had once enjoyed seemed like I might have dreamed them. But I had a home court advantage that eventually helped me win.

If my girlfriend hadn't been in my corner and in the driver's seat, I might not have made it. If my son hadn't provided the lifeblood for my persistence, I might not have made it. If my friend hadn't opened her home, her kitchen, and her memory books to me, I might not have made it.

There were so many people who were crucial in carrying me along the path until I could find my footing once again. They were like roadside assistance on a road trip that I wasn't sure I would survive. It's because of them that I was able to hang on and continue to push myself forward when all I heard and received were rejections and nos. They kept me fueled and running until that final, beautiful yes arrived.

The painful irony of rejection and acceptance is that we only need one yes. One is all it takes but getting there can mean a mailbox full of rejection letters from colleges, a dozen "we're not interested" replies from potential employers, or, like Stephen King experienced, manuscript rejections from thirty different publishers. Along the way though, wielding your home court advantage will make all the difference.

> The painful irony of rejection and acceptance is that we only need one yes.

If you're waiting for the right opportunity or feel like *no* is the only word you hear, take heart knowing that it doesn't necessarily mean you're on the wrong path. You might be on your tenth job interview, and maybe, like me, you got dressed for success while standing in the Ritz Carlton parking lot after sleeping in your car. In those moments, remember: It only takes one yes.

— CHAPTER 3 —

Be Relentless

YOU KNOW THAT feeling when you want something so desperately that you're willing to push yourself and your limits to get it? Maybe it's prompted by dire situations, such as an investor who put a second mortgage on his house in order to chase his big dream, or by silly competitions and the need to win, like driving across state lines to prove to a friend that your favorite restaurant is, in fact, the best barbecue joint around.

We were born with the urge to come out on top. When we're little, it's in our DNA to take what we believe is ours. You know this is true. If you don't believe me, spend five minutes watching a couple of two-year-old children play together with a limited number of toys. It doesn't matter who brought the toy, who deserves the toy, or who should have the toy. The toddler who wants the toy the *most* always wins. Toddlers don't approach negotiations obsessing about their past failures or whether or not they were able to come out of playgroup victoriously holding onto a toy the last time they played with their friends. Little kids just listen to their gut, and their gut almost always tells them that whatever they want automatically belongs to them. They take the things they want, and they scream "Mine!" without stopping to wonder if they deserve it or not.

Adulthood whittles away that fierce emotion and confident level of ownership in positive ways, as we lean into politeness and kindness, but it can also take away the fierce drive we need to hold our place on the leaderboard. That doesn't mean we should steal from others at all costs, but it does mean that we should believe we have a right to fight for something when we follow appropriate and integrity-filled methods to obtain it. Without becoming selfish and entitled, we can learn to harness that primal drive to own and win that was preprogrammed into us as children and develop it in healthy ways so that it manifests as success that doesn't harm others.

Whether we've felt that deep-down burning desire to win as a player on the football field or as a fan in the stands, in the board room as the CEO or on the sales floor as a new recruit, we know what it feels like to be consumed with the idea of winning and the drive to come out on top. In those instances, it's not that we *want* to win, but rather that we *need* to win.

You may be reading this and feel like that heightened sense of staying ahead of the pack is your normal. Constant competition is your happy place, and your natural state might be argumentative to a fault and driven to win at all costs. Your friends probably describe you as "overly competitive" during board games or tailgate parties.

Or you might be on the opposite end of that spectrum, where rivalry of any kind makes you feel queasy, and speaking up for yourself or using new methods to attack a problem from every angle feels foreign and risky. Even if competition of any kind has you running for shelter, there has undoubtedly been at least one time in your past when you felt that fire in your belly that you couldn't deny. The kind that made you stand up to the school bully. The hunger that made you beat everyone to the finish line. The desperation that willed you to step further outside of your comfort zone than you ever had before to protect or defend a belief or a family member or a way of life. A fire that led you to run faster or get up earlier or think more critically.

I've worked closely with hundreds of different personalities over the last few decades, and I've witnessed what type of person rakes in success more than others. Without question, I can tell you that it is not necessarily experience or charisma that puts a salesperson at the top of the leaderboard. It's remarkable to me that the person everyone seems to have a magnetic connection to doesn't always win, and the guy with decades' worth of tenure doesn't always come out on top. Rather, time and time again, regardless of market region or product category, I have seen that the person who possesses an unrelenting drive to win will over time consistently make more sales and climb ahead on the leaderboard.

> *...the person who possesses an unrelenting drive to win will over time consistently make more sales and climb ahead on the leaderboard.*

A Customer Saying Yes Means You Don't Have to Say No

As I work with teams, the mantra I teach and encourage my employees to memorize is that if you can get a customer to say yes, you won't have to tell your family no. When I get a yes from a customer, it means I can provide something else for my family. There have been years when a yes meant I could buy groceries that week and put food on the table. Thankfully, there have been a lot of years where a yes meant one more lavish extravagance I could bless my family with or the ability to generously share with others who aren't in the same boat. If I settle for a no from a customer and easily back down, it lessens my options, limits my resources, and keeps me from providing for the needs and wants of my family and even my community. That burden is on my shoulders at all times. I felt it every time I walked out on that showroom floor in those early years and still feel it today. If I give up and give in easily whenever I meet resistance from a potential buyer or client, I have to face the music when I look at our family budget or bank account. The number of times I settle for a rejection is reflected pretty plainly in those numbers. And the numbers don't lie.

I always have those numbers and needs hovering just above me, urging me to keep pushing, but they are multiplied exponentially by my innate need

> *if you can get a customer to say yes, you won't have to tell your family no.*

to come out on top in every competition I find myself in. I'm driven to provide for my family, but I'm also driven to prove the critical voices in my head wrong. We all have them from time to time. We all want to make people proud of us too. I want to give my father something to be proud of almost as much as I want a new luxury vehicle or indulgent vacation. I'm driven when I think about how high I climbed as a multi-millionaire, but I'm equally motivated when I'm reminded how desperately low I sank in 2008. I'm on constant alert so I can prevent myself from slipping into complacency.

Those pressures can be suffocating at times, but when regulated and wielded effectively, those same pressures we put on ourselves can make us better and more successful. They make us willing to vulnerably stick our necks out in discomfort and push beyond our own natural safety zones and barriers. They inspire us to go through a metamorphosis of change and transition from push-overs and fearful followers to calculated risk takers and courageous leaders. But it is powerful to remember that even as we succeed, the growth and drive must never stop if we're to continue reaching our highest potential.

Our move to New York came at the right time. On paper, it appeared that I had not compromised my professional trajectory, which was very important to me. The money was good, although not near what I had earned as Partner. The timing was obviously perfect, given that I had lost everything and was desperately seeking a way to feed my family, while also pushing my career in the direction I had envisioned. The reason and season of the opportunity was perfect. But as I worked and pushed in my new role in New York, I knew that returning to my status as Partner would be a longshot. That kind of move was not going to be probable with the gentleman I worked for there. Even though my title looked good on paper, the role wasn't shiny like the ones I had held prior. If I was going to keep climbing, I was going to have to keep pushing—even if it meant spearheading something I had never done before.

At the time, a seed had been planted in my head to one day live in California and enjoy the ocean. As I worked in New York, I began investigating and researching a guy on the opposite coast who was an incredible businessman. Under his leadership, his dealership became the number one Honda dealer in the world and his leadership style was efficient and unmatched. He described his operation as the Nordstrom of the car business, and I began hearing buzz that he was interested in growing his business outside of the state of California. To do this, he needed someone with experience operating outside of the state, but I also discovered that he was looking for a minority candidate based on whispers I'd heard from the National Association for Minority Dealers.

In that moment, even though I had a secure job and no one from the outside looking in would have thought I needed a job change, I saw my next step. After meeting with this California owner multiple times, we moved from the New York and New Jersey market to the west coast where I would lead his expansion plans. In a few short years, I went from basically bankrupt to living in Newport Beach as the Director of Operations for a major auto group.

Had I decided that comfortable and safe were enough, I never would have known the thrill of blazing a new trail and building something from scratch—not to mention the drastic boost in pay. But even these moments of victory were not easy. Working in this slick, well-run organization that had held the number one ranking in the world for over two decades didn't come without its challenges. Never in my life have I arrived at a job and felt like I could sit back and enjoy the ride. In this new role, like the many others that came before it, I had to create my own worth, my own agenda, and my own way to make a difference.

In a few short years, I went from basically bankrupt to living in Newport Beach as the Director of Operations for a major auto group.

Expanding outside of California meant identifying and applying for open points, or available markets for new dealerships. We discovered a Toyota open point in Texas and began the process of trying to secure it, which included working with the owner and the Chief Operating Officer to present our business plan in a boardroom in front of 20 Toyota executives. I was an experienced salesman and leader, but I had never made a big presentation like this before in my life.

Over two hundred applicants threw their hat in the ring. From there, the Toyota team whittled the number down to 50, then 20, and then three. There is nothing else in the world that can provide the same eerie feeling as preparing a PowerPoint presentation that includes everything you have ever accomplished, hoped, and dreamed for, and then clicking through the slides in a fluorescent-lit boardroom filled with people who hold the next potential goal for your career in their hands.

This was about me making a difference but, more than anything else, this role would be an opportunity for me to become a dealer, which was what I was really chasing. It was the underlying reason why I moved to California in the first place. All the jobs before this one had provided money and credibility and helped me make a name for myself. All the other roles were just appetizers. This opportunity was the main dish.

The owner received a call from one of the Toyota executives that, confidentially, we were it, the chosen ones. We had felt good about our presentation and the connection we made with the leaders in that room, but his words were that extra push that let us know we had nailed it. With our confidence and his off-the-record words, we just knew we were shoe-ins. We didn't put our house on the market or anything immediate, but I was confident that this was the next step.

Then word came that I was wrong: The dealership opening was awarded to another group. It was a huge feeling of defeat and extremely disappointing. I thought we had won it. I thought what I had presented was more than enough, but ultimately it was not ours for the taking. The feeling echoed what I had felt in 2008, like it was all coming back to me. I was right back in that moment where it was all slipping away. So much had been riding on that new development, and the position I held at the auto group in California had been created as a place marker for me until we gained a new dealership out of state. Now, I wasn't even sure if I had a job at all.

I ended up leaving California with a difficult feeling in my chest and a lump in my throat. This had been my shot to get back to where I needed and wanted to be. It had all been right there in front of me, and then it didn't work out. It felt like the rug had been ripped out from under me.

Get Comfortable with Being Uncomfortable

This lost opportunity felt so large that it didn't seem like a singular disappointment, but rather a combination of all of my losses. It was as if this one missed opportunity dredged up every previous failure and misstep from my past. I was grieving not winning the Texas dealership, but in reality, I was grieving all the other missed opportunities—from dropping that football in elementary school to bankrupting my dreams and my bank account in 2008. The loss of the idea, vision, and goal I had before me seemed to evaporate as well. Suddenly, I wasn't just despairing over what might have been in Texas, I was commiserating over it all. The loss felt so great that finding the momentum to keep moving forward became even harder. The boulder of success that I was pushing uphill seemed to double in size, and giving up became more attractive than I ever thought possible.

These are the moments when it's the easiest to throw in the towel. When you're right on the cusp of greatness and it all falls apart, I've found that it feels easier to give up. It's this strange paradox because you've come farther than you have ever managed to go before. But when you stumble a few feet from the goal, the embarrassment and second guessing is infinitely stronger. The closer you are to the finish line, the easier it can be to give up. You did try, after all. To those around you, you're still a hero for putting yourself out there. No one could look at how much you gave, how hard you worked and the time you sacrificed and think you were lazy. You showed up and left it all out on the field and it didn't work out, so it seems natural to assume that the big win, the huge achievement, the success and dream you had been working toward just isn't in the cards for you.

This is why I came up with this catchphrase that I keep on repeat when I'm working with leaders and training teams: *Become comfortable with being* *unc*omfortable. Even losing can become comfortable when it's what we expect. You've heard winning is contagious, but in my experience, losing can become a virus that turns into a chronic illness. It can almost begin to feel like a curse. When someone has failed so many times in a row, they can be tempted to just continue to fail and accept it as their fate.

This is the same feeling that can haunt us when we battle with alcohol or gambling addictions. Those tendencies and vices are always just beneath the surface, threatening to peek their heads out at any moment and show back up. It's common sense that we must rebuke addiction temptations when they appear. We don't work diligently to get sober and then spend weekends in a bar. When we want to overcome something that can so powerfully manipulate our minds and actions, we get the stumbling blocks out of our lives and steer clear of our triggers because the consequences of giving in and falling back into the rhythm of addiction are too great.

> *You've heard winning is contagious, but in my experience, losing can become a virus that turns into a chronic illness.*

I see failure the same way. It's always lurking, willing us to quit and become complacent or tuck our tails and run. If we do, we may never know how shockingly large the losses are. We need to acknowledge the potential of "what might have been" that we throw away in the process of walking away. We're familiar with the saying, "You'll never know if you don't try." Most people hear that and think about their own potential that isn't being tapped. My gut takes that one step further, contemplating all the missed experiences—both wins and failures—that people never get a chance to learn from because their string of losses has made them too scared to put themselves out there.

Les Brown has been an incredible mentor to me, as I have continued to strive toward my dreams. Starting from nothing and labeled by early educators as mentally retarded, Les went on to become a sought-after keynote speaker who attracts audiences of 80,000 people and was voted by Toastmasters International as one of the Top Five Outstanding Speakers. His message and book, *It's Not Over Until You Win,* has been transformative for me and is one of the reasons I have been able to press beyond failure toward my goals.

His daughter, Ona Brown, who is the owner of World Impact Now and a renowned speaker in her own right, has been an incredible friend, like a sister to me over the years. I was honored to be mentioned in her book and she always encouraged me to continue believing in my dreams.

For decades, both Les and Ona have been training people to understand that even if you don't have what you want today, it's possible to keep dreaming.

It's possible to keep working toward your goals daily even in the midst of heavy disappointments and setbacks. The key is to keep working toward those dreams daily and be willing to take a chance. It's in this process of working through and past disappointments that we can discover the greatness within us.

When I consider stopping or quitting, I can hear Ona's voice in my head: *You're more powerful than you have ever imagined.* Just because I hear a no from a potential investor or employer, that's not the finish line for me. Someone else's opinion of my ability does not have to become my reality. I can choose to never stop growing, stretching, and working on myself, even if failure keeps knocking me down. The irony and beauty of defeat is that it teaches you more than winning ever could. Defeat shows you where to improve, what muscles to build and flex and how your message is being received, for better or for worse.

When I was a kid working alongside my dad, I had plenty of these learning moments. Barely a teenager, detailing cars was a boring chore, but I learned quickly how important it was that I perform well. Over the summer, my dad would give me one of the old, torn-up cars from the back of the junk lot to clean. No amount of work would have enabled these cars to run, but it was my responsibility to clean them up. Whatever I sold the junker for, my dad explained, would be the amount of money I had to buy school clothes with. If I sold it for $200, I'd have $200 worth of school clothes. If I couldn't sell it, I'd have to show up to school the next year with jeans that didn't quite fit and shoes that had seen better days.

These junk cars were piled in the back of the lot for a reason: No one wanted them. To be handed one and then told it would be the sole source of funding for my style and reputation at school felt like a loss from the very beginning. But I kept working and looking for an angle that would help me sell them anyway. This challenge was my first introduction to selling cars, and since I'd started cleaning them at such a young age, I knew how to make them look good. My biggest sale when it came to those school clothes cars was $375. It was a good year for my closet.

Even when the odds are stacked against you, even when you've been handed a task that has set you up for failure, remember that you are greater than your defeats. It is imperative that you continue to fuel your momentum and drive as you move toward your dreams. Otherwise, your vision for where you want to end up may never even hit your horizon line. You have to keep moving in the direction of your dreams without concern for failure because failure isn't permanent. Giving up will not be an option when you are driven by the desire to win.

But living with this relentless energy for pursuing your dreams means your day-to-day life might need to look different than what you're used to. If we refuse to give in to the ease of quitting and fight back diligently against accepting defeat as our normal, we must become comfortable with being uncomfortable in other areas.

When we decide to take big risks, like chasing down our goals or taking on new challenges like a scary cross-country job change, we will undoubtedly experience a rush of anxiety. That's human nature. It's our body's way of protecting us from something that could potentially harm us. When something is new instead of normal, our adrenaline kicks in, urging us to fight against what's upset our rhythm and put us back into that safety zone we're used to. Yet, if we'll allow ourselves to push past the initial fear, there is often something even better on the other side of it.

If we want to move in a direction that is against the status quo, if we want to make something more with our lives, we'll have to allow ourselves to feel that discomfort, push past it, and move into the unknown. The brilliant part about pushing yourself into the unknown is that eventually it becomes a known. When you move into the uncertainty outside of your comfort zone, eventually that scary spot can develop its own level of comfort. New jobs eventually become old ones or ones we've had for years. New relationships become the go-to person we call when something big happens. But none of those new rewarding comfort zones can be created without leaving the old ones. You can't gain yardage if you're too scared to get off the bench.

Shaking Up Your Day-to-Day

When I was 14 and living in Las Vegas with my dad, he would keep his used cars at the Caesar's Palace valet parking lot overnight until our dealership would open in the morning. One day, my dad tasked me with finding a way to sell one of those cars. At 14, with no phone and no money, selling a used car was a bit of a challenge. But I knew how to work the angles in a sale and how to make a car look good. And arguing with my dad would have been futile.

Calling on all the times I'd worked behind the scenes to help my dad get close to a sale, I remembered putting cars in the paper as a way to get attention. I had put advertisements for used cars in the *Dallas Morning News* or the *Fort Worth Herald* throughout childhood. And back then, the paper would bill you based on your phone number. If your phone number had a good history of payment, they would put the ad in the paper and then send an invoice to you that you could pay later. I knew the *Las Vegas Sun* would be the same way. I went down to the operator at the casino where we were staying and said, "Hey, could you help me? I'm going to put an ad in the paper for a few cars that I have here to sell, and I just need you to transfer the calls to my room." The operator looked at me, a 14-year-old kid, and obviously said no. I thought long and hard about what options I had. My dad told me I had to figure out a way to get these cars sold, but doing that as a minor and with basically no earthly belongings or means of communication would be tricky.

As I paced in the casino lobby, I remembered there was a 7-11 gas station next door. A gas station pay phone, I knew, would have a recorded history of paid phone bills. I picked the car I knew would get the most attention, a Lincoln Town Car limousine, and listed the phone number as the 7-11 pay phone for the newspaper advertisement. I backed the limo up to the pay phone and every time the phone rang, I would run to it and answer like it was my own personal phone number.

Las Vegas is one of those strange places in the world where a 14-year-old driving a limo and answering phone calls from a pay phone isn't the oddest thing a person can see in a day. Sure enough, a gentleman drove in from Arizona to buy the limo, and we made $10,000 off the sale. Selling a used limo from a 7-11 pay phone off the side of Caesar's Palace was one of those "good job" pat on the backs I got from my dad.

The way we've always done things isn't always the best way. There were a million reasons why I shouldn't have been able to sell that limo. I was underage, underfunded, and had very few resources at my disposal. But I had drive and courage and the willingness to switch things up and try a new strategy to make a sale. Sometimes that means selling a limo from a gas station pay phone outside of a casino. Not every sale or win will come from relying on the same template. And after living through the many exhausting and difficult ways I have found buyers, that's a relief!

If we're playing to win, we have to be creative, inventive, and unafraid to put ourselves out there. At 14, selling used cars from a pay phone didn't exactly win me style points with the popular crowd, but it did teach me how to be comfortable with awkward and new business ventures. It taught me how to work around the immovable limitations that were handed to me, and it taught me how to sell a car to just about anybody. That strange teenage win helped me prepare for an even bigger one down the road.

Shaking up your day-to-day is the best way to acclimate yourself and get comfortable with the uncomfortable. If you thrive on routine, train yourself to try something different at least once a week. Get coffee somewhere new, reach out to a colleague further ahead of you in your industry, flip-flop your afternoon schedule with your morning one. Little shifts will prepare your personality and mindset for unexpected challenges that are bound to occur. When you get accustomed to change in small ways, big changes won't be so earth shaking. Then try bigger changes on for size when the chance arises: a job change, a new hobby, an unusual wardrobe style you thought was too risky, or a new workout routine.

> *Shaking up your day-to-day is the best way to acclimate yourself and get comfortable with the uncomfortable.*

Failure is scary, and rejections are discouraging. I understand. I've hit the finish line second (or last) and considered giving up, too. I've also been to the other side of that failure, and I can tell you that when you experience those types of losses, when you fail spectacularly and feel the crushing weight of disappointment, you are closer to your dream than you have ever been before. If I had given up at any point on my road, I would have missed the incredible views from the mountaintops of success that waited just around the corner from my last failure or rejection. We have to keep trying and challenging ourselves. Dreams don't come easy, but for those who play to win, they do come true.

— CHAPTER 4 —

Be Audible Ready

REGARDLESS OF WHERE I work, it is always important to me to keep a sparkling reputation. The auto sales industry is vast and spread out, but dealers and corporate executives talk. I always want to make sure that I keep my word about everything I say I will do. Part of that is due to my desire for integrity, of course, but I'm also well aware that careers and industries constantly fluctuate. A stable, secure job today might be gone tomorrow, and I need to be ready to change course at all times. Even if my particular job remains secure, there are going to be opportunities every single day when I can change my focus or alter my routine in ways that are necessary to stay at the front of the pack. I prepare for what I know to be true for now but keep my eyes on the horizon, so I can shift and adjust as necessary.

This readiness is common in sports, where plays and defensive structures rapidly evolve with each down, timeout, or half. In football, this is especially important. Plays are drawn out on whiteboards in the locker room, rehearsed during practice, and confirmed in the huddle. But when a quarterback gets to the line, everything can be changed with one or two words shouted over a center's back as he surveys the arrangement of defensive linemen or an open pocket on the field that no one else has noticed.

These rapid changes of play called out unexpectedly by the quarterback are known as audibles. Every member of the team leaves the team huddle on the sidelines with a certain play in mind, but once they hit the line of scrimmage, their ears are open, listening to discern what play will actually be happening.

Peyton Manning's "Omaha" battle cry is one of the most well-known audible play calls in NFL history. Gifs and memes of him standing at the line urgently shouting "Omaha" to his teammates have become part of pop culture now, and that one word and image of Manning is now used to convey the idea that whatever plan had been in place before would now rapidly need to change. Although he was very secretive about it until after he retired, Manning revealed in March of 2017 that his signature "Omaha" yell was an indicator word that he used to signal to his team that the clock was low, the play had changed, and he needed the ball snapped immediately.

Football isn't the only arena where audibles are necessary. Any business that plans to survive the changes in customer demands, unforeseen economic turmoil, and surprising market upheavals must master the ability to recognize the need for a sudden shift in direction. Learning to call an audible with confidence, and then effectively direct a team or organization to rapidly move to accommodate the change, is imperative for successful and thriving organizations.

But any group, company, or team that isn't willing to budge on their established plans even when the climate and game has shifted around them, should prepare for defeat. This may not happen overnight. Businesses don't crumble in one day, and people don't wake up one morning to realize that their lives went in the wrong direction in a single sleep. There are warning signs along the road that, if we are alert enough to notice, can prompt us to make a U-turn, find a detour, or stop and ask for directions.

Depending on the type of business or team you're in, these warnings can look like customers whose loyalties have begun to drift to another brand of marketing style, or a spouse who becomes increasingly more distant or cold. If we are willing to own up to our part in failures that loom on the horizon, we can be audible ready. If we are willing to acknowledge the evolution of relationships or the market and see that what has always worked in the past may not work in the future, we can be audible ready. When we plant our feet and dig our heels into the soil of our past wins, refusing to move, we're simply choosing the ground for our company or team or relationship to die on.

Our tendency is to continue trying to force the pieces until they make a perfect fit, even when life feels like a square peg in a round hole. If, instead, we will look down and realize that our approach isn't correct, we can call an audible and address the problem rather than pretend it will simply work itself out in the end. On the relationship front, calling an audible could mean choosing to spend more time at home with your family or committing to attend counseling. At work, it may mean painful power shifts in management or difficult choices to drastically reduce overhead.

When we plant our feet and dig our heels into the soil of our past wins, refusing to move, we're simply choosing the ground for our company or team or relationship to die on.

If your life or business aren't headed in the right direction, don't look sideways for a place to lay blame; look at your roadmap. Consider what choices led you to this moment of uncertainty or instability and what choices could lead you out. And if things are moving smoothly, what changes could you implement in the future to make sure you don't accidentally merge off the path into areas that will hurt your profit margin or sink your relationships?

Learning from Others' Mistakes

The retail space is full of stories of mom-and-pop stores and homegrown businesses that didn't fully understand the market they were entering or prepare properly and sank before they were given a fighting chance. But the corporate world is just as rampant with stories of giant conglomerates who refused to switch gears and ultimately were forced to close their doors. These household names covered their ears, refusing to listen to the advice of market or industry analysts and tuned out customers who were telling them with their feet and pocketbooks that the times were changing. For these companies, defiantly staying on the trail they had blazed and clinging to their past wins as proof that they didn't need to deviate from their plans eventually led them to a dead-end road they could not recover from.

Many of the giants who enjoyed the wealth that the '80s had to offer found themselves drowning when technology changed the game in the new millennium. Instead of being the industry leaders, they were chasing the competition down the very trail they themselves had cleared. We've watched as Dell and Sony went from disrupting their markets with PCs that cut out the middle man and Walkmans that were as abundant a few decades ago as the smartphone is today, to running to catch up to their innovative competitors. We witnessed stores like Eastman Kodak and Radio Shack fail to modernize in step with the advancing trends and technology until they ultimately dissolved into the background. We gobbled up the cool Motorola Razr phone in 2003 but then switched loyalty as Motorola floundered in its smartphone development. Almost all of us had an AOL, Hotmail, or Yahoo email account until their clunky systems were outpaced and their security measures were called into question.

Some brands seem too big to fail, but that's what can actually turn out to be a company's biggest weakness. Blockbuster was one of those household names who allowed their greatest weakness to turn into their greatest nightmare. Famous for its brick-and-mortar video rental concept, Blockbuster was the go-to source for home entertainment before videos and movies could be streamed on Roku, Apple TV, and almost any smartphone. I still remember stopping at Blockbuster on my way home from work to rent something for the weekend, slowly combing through their new releases section to spy a new movie I hadn't yet watched. Even if a movie was really popular, each store only had so many copies, so if you got there too late on a Friday night, your options would consist of whatever B-movies the renters before you had left behind. It was a system that worked perfectly for many years. Blockbuster was the center of entertainment throughout the '80s and '90s, and we were loyal customers who flocked to it on the weekends or when we had to stay home sick from work or school.

But entertainment began to evolve, and customers found other ways to watch, like having DVDs mailed to their home by Netflix, watching videos on-demand through their cable providers, and renting DVDs for a buck from vending machine retailers like Redbox. Recognizing their opportunity but still holding only a sliver of the market share, Netflix approached Blockbuster in 2000, offering to sell their company to the Hercules of the entertainment industry for $50 million. The CEO of Blockbuster refused, scoffing at Netflix, which he believed to be a niche company that was losing money.

Of course, we know the end of the story. Slowly, we watched ourselves and others migrate from the video store experience to a Netflix subscription. Blockbuster tried to recalibrate, offering the same DVD by mail subscription service, but the battle was already too far gone. The company declared bankruptcy in 2010, and this generation of kids doesn't have any concept of walking into a video store to rent a movie.

Today, Netflix has over 100 million subscribers and over $8 billion in revenue. With a fresh understanding of the market, they turned their sliver of market share into a powerhouse and left Blockbuster reeling in a wake of remorse.

It's easy in retrospect to see Blockbuster's obvious missteps because we have the fortunate position to see the whole picture in our rearview mirrors and are easily able to call out their gaffes. We get to be armchair quarterbacks who point out their unwillingness to innovate and their comfort with a stagnant system. In real time, these potential blunders were not marked with giant road blocks or yellow caution tape, of course. Yet, anyone who was attuned to the pulse of customer interests and paradigm shifts in the market, and was willing to accept the changes happening around them, could have seen trouble looming.

Like Blockbuster, Toys R Us also became too comfortable with their success. As the premier toy seller in the United States in the '90s, Toys R Us and its "I don't wanna grow up, I'm a Toys R Us kid" jingle had celebrity status. It was known for being the go-to place for Christmas toy shopping and in its heyday was responsible for shutting down smaller chains who couldn't compete. With so much padding in their expansive customer base and excellent brand recognition, the company enjoyed many years of invincibility. That success, however, eventually rendered them unable to recognize their own fragility.

By the late '90s, Walmart became the toy store's biggest competitor, and in 1998 the big box store overtook the specialty store as the number one toy seller in the country. Toys R Us didn't go down without a fight. In 2005, they sought out investors to take the company private, but since the company was basically bought with its own equity, the brand was now the holder of a ridiculous amount of debt that topped $5 billion. That debt meant they couldn't be flexible, and while Target, Amazon, and Walmart were able to pour their resources into customer experience and e-commerce trends, Toys R Us was using what little budgetary discretion it had to simply gasp for air.

The saddest part of this downfall is that the corporate leaders of Toys R Us probably believed they were trying their best to innovate. Looking across the toy landscape, they realized they needed help with their online sales, so they signed a 10-year contract with Amazon to become the e-commerce giant's exclusive toy vendor. But Amazon didn't hold up their end of the bargain. After Toys R Us sued to end their contract in 2004, they were left with an online presence that was meager compared to their online retail competitors and too many years behind the trend. Instead of investing in themselves, they had handed their online future over to someone else.

Ironically, Target had a similar experience, but when they prematurely ended their contract with Amazon, they invested $2.5 billion per year to enhance their online site. Toys R Us, on the other hand, who was extremely overdue in creating their online presence, dedicated only $100 million over a three-year span to revamping their website. The company would go on to die

> *Toys R Us and Blockbuster both failed to acknowledge the wins of their competitors.*

a slow death over the next decade, but it never overcame the early missteps that happened while it was still enjoying the popularity and profit of its heyday.

Toys R Us and Blockbuster both failed to acknowledge the wins of their competitors. If Toys R Us had taken notes from the up-and-coming major players in its market, like Walmart, they would have recognized that in order to keep up, they would have to offer multi-genre product lines. Walmart was a beast in the toy market because of its loss leaders and slimmer profit margins on the toy aisle that it was only able to swallow because of profit margins that could be made up in other places throughout the store. If Blockbuster would have looked up from its own success and acknowledged a shifting technology landscape, they would have had the foresight to partner with companies who were ahead of trends.

These types of innovations require not only discomfort and unease—and maybe even a level of anxiety—but also the humility necessary to accept that you don't have it all figured out. That kind of perspective can be difficult when you've been the one leading the way and serving as the standard for excellence for everyone else for decades. You may be the top tier executive or the leading salesperson today, but if you think your work is done simply because you've reached the top, you have deceived yourself.

It is not humiliating to call an audible. It's not a poor sign of leadership to look out over the field and see that things have changed in ways you couldn't have anticipated and make a judgment call at the last minute. Poor leadership means scanning the field with a critical eye, noting any threats or challenges, and being too embarrassed, scared, or prideful to shout out the important changes that can keep you or your team afloat. Strong leadership means making the tough judgement calls and taking the flak that comes with them in order to protect the entire ship from sinking.

Success Resides on the Other Side of Scary

There's something inherently scary about trying something new or branching out to a different market, product genre, or sales pitch. But success often resides on the other side of scary.

I've moved across the country more than once to take a challenging leadership role. At one point, I moved to Texas to serve as president of 20 AutoNation dealerships. As the leader for hundreds of employees, I was responsible for protecting the company's assets and growing the people.

When you're in top-tier leadership, its common to bring in your own team, but I found that recruiting during that season for the company wasn't the right move. So when I walked in on day one, I knew I had to win with the players

I had been dealt. To do that, we started with a very thorough strengths and weaknesses analysis of each leader. This system allowed me to identify what a win looked like for each leader and how I could make a contribution to their business. This was so important because wins are relative. What looks like a lot of money or success is drastically different from person to person.

I hear people say, "Just do your best," but doing your best can get you fired if it's not enough for your employer or client. Through that analysis, we identified what was working and what wasn't, and then it was my responsibility to make sure the leader wasn't selling themselves short somewhere. I helped them define what good looked like and then adjust their expectations, their systems, their routines, and their techniques so they could reach higher and win bigger. Knowing where you're lacking and where you're killing it is imperative for growth to happen. Once you know these basic building blocks, it's easier to call an audible, reset your focus and hit the ground running.

Sometimes I can lay out a solution for a leader I'm working with that has been proven, tested, and tried with other brands who have similar demographics for their customer base. When that happens, I know it's a proven play that can run a lot of times. For these types of actions, it comes down to execution of the play, and I believe wholeheartedly in modeling what that execution looks like.

> *Knowing where you're lacking and where you're killing it is imperative for growth to happen.*

I like to spend time with each leader and help them learn to set their own daily instrument panel. To do this, I'll write what I call a prescription. That prescription is how to arrange and execute their day, so they know what good looks like every day and how to reach it. If people want to massage it a bit so it fits within their personality or routine, that's fine, but I want the sandbox to stay pretty much the same. As their business gets healthier, I'm happy to talk about how to dial that prescription back. Until then, I expect them to religiously follow each piece of the daily action plan.

Occasionally I will meet with a store or franchise leader who responds to me with apathy or even resentment that I would attempt to show them ways they could improve. What I tell them is that *If you didn't need a doctor, I wouldn't be here to help you get well.* If they didn't need a new prescription for how to improve their approach to sales, I wouldn't have been asked to provide them with one. Accepting that kind of targeted guidance from someone who is further down the road from you in age or experience is an important part of success. Sometimes you don't know enough or haven't experienced enough to be able to look down the field and notice the changes or see the shift in the defensive line. It can be tempting when things are going well to fool yourself into thinking, just like Blockbuster and Toys R Us did, that everything is fine, and adjustments are unnecessary. Sometimes you need to call in someone with a little more experience or education to call the audible for you. If you don't have anyone like that in your life, let this book be that for you.

To give you an even better picture of what a winning prescription looks like, I'll share the highlights of a prescription I give to my leaders in the car business as an example. Although it's specific to our line of work, the intention and process translates to just about any other trade or leadership role as well.

In our industry, winning has everything to do with how you open your business and how you put it to sleep. We start very early with a morning team meeting so we can look at our wins and opportunities from the day before, much like a football team goes over films from previous games to see where they need to tighten up and where they could run the ball. This allows us to create a daily strategic plan of what the day is going to look like for each teammate, without accidentally overlapping responsibilities or wasting the energy of two people on a task that could be accomplished by one. We break up our day into minutes and put what I call timestamps on everything we do. We decide what's going to happen at ten o'clock, eleven o'clock and so on. That way, if we get off track, we all know the game plan we should be on, and since we have instilled a strong sense of urgency in that morning team meeting, anyone can have the opportunity to quickly jump back into the play because they know what should be happening and when. I'm hyper-focused in laying out every detail because detail is retail, and you can't be a leader in retail without them.

This is also the time when we set what I call our "instrument panels." Leading an organization is like teaching a team to drive a fleet of Ferraris.

I want to make sure that all of our instrument panels—our fuel levels, RPM's, miles per hour—are all the same. I want our motivations, drive, and speed to match so that we can identify what winning looks like. When we do that and identify what is most important to us as a team, it helps us understand where to place our urgency. This keeps us from drifting midday into tasks that don't contribute to the overall goal of the team. It ensures that the things that matter the most don't fall at the mercy of the things that matter the least.

Closing out the day strong is just as important as how you start. For my teams, that means a checkout process. Before anyone goes home, they have to check in with their supervisor and go over their checkout sheet that details how their day went. The sheet shows how many people they talked to that day, how many sales they made, and what they expect for tomorrow. This quick check-in catches patterns of failure, but it also prevents failure before it happens because it can be seen on the horizon before it arrives.

This closing practice each day is important for companies to succeed on a macro level, but it's also important to me personally because I know that when employees lose, they take it home to their families. As failures snowball, they tend to affect a person's home life, and I believe it's a manager's responsibility to make sure they know what their employee's home life is like. Losses at work can equal losses at home, and we have the opportunity and responsibility to help fix those patterns before they become so engrained and severe that they go beyond something we can fix. We, as leaders, can have a generational impact simply by helping someone improve their daily sales quotas. When we look at each leader's success from a bird's eye view and track their strategies and patterns, we're able to help them win, which helps families win, which can ultimately impact the lives of dozens if not hundreds of people. The simple checkout process has that kind of power, and it's why it's such a vital part of the prescription.

The checkout sheets are practical because they allow us to make appointments today to win tomorrow. They flash warning signs if an employee isn't succeeding or making plans to win, and they prevent employee turnover and the slow seepage of profit losses that occur over time. These process-driven techniques allow leaders to catch seemingly insignificant acts—like a low customer interaction rate for a few days in a row—as they develop so that they won't go unnoticed, eventually accumulate, and translate to big losses.

When these detrimental patterns of action or thinking begin to develop, these daily prescriptions give leaders the information they need so they're equipped and empowered to call an audible before it's too late. Underachievers on the team are quickly identified, and managers have the time and space to discern whether their lack of results can be turned around through training or if the employee is simply slacking off and needs to be eliminated from the team altogether. Most importantly, following this prescription of team meetings, timestamps, and checkout sheets gives your team the tangible resources it needs to consistently win.

I've applied this prescription to my own life, and I can tell you that sometimes I have had to change in ways I wasn't expecting. The biggest priority for me is ensuring that the best part of my life is in the windshield, not in the rearview mirror.

Clearly, in 2008 and 2009, when my career crumbled and absolutely fell apart to the point where I was sleeping in my girlfriend's car and relying on the generosity of other people to help me pull through, my clear and defined trajectory was in jeopardy. My dream of having a legacy as an automotive dealer was at stake. I wanted to be a leader in the automotive industry, a pillar in my community, and someone who could truly make a difference, but all of that required making changes that were difficult at times and frequently when I wasn't sure I was ready. The biggest audibles I have made relate to those moments when I could see my trajectory failing and I could feel myself slipping dangerously off the path I had cleared for myself. I want to wake up in the morning and determine what I want my day to look like, to choose when I go to sleep at night, to determine how many sick days I am allowed to have, and to be in control of my own life. I want the boss to be in the mirror for me. I put a lot of pressure on myself, but that pressure keeps me calling audibles without hinderance whenever I see those goals and priorities start to fade away.

I love helping businesses and leaders discover where they need to shore up their weaknesses. It's a blessing to me when I can help a dealer or salesperson tweak their choices and techniques in a positive direction that can benefit every aspect of their life.

Using my prescription for daily routines, morning meetings, timestamps and checkouts, I was able to help dealerships develop a much more intelligent day-to-day approach. We took the opportunities for growth that we discovered together through a detailed strength and weakness analysis and discovered how those could make a contribution to their business. Together, we found a way to win.

Results come from following a plan and working hard. If you eat right and work out, your body is going to show the results of that effort. Business is the same way. I've watched salespeople refuse help or guidance, and I've sat on the sidelines as their careers dissolved. Much like mega-corporations that can't see the plays changing on the economic or market landscape in front of them, these prideful employees preferred holding their course, doing things the way they had always been done, and their futures suffered for it.

Sometimes the problem is not that they don't know what they should do, but rather they refuse to put the plan into action. But I've also watched this play unfold in real time in the lives of countless people I've mentored, and I have watched the results roll in on checkout sheets, sales numbers, profit margins, happy home lives, and contentment in leadership.

Being audible-ready means never settling for status quo and continually looking for opportunities to grow, change, stretch, and share. If we're refusing to grow stagnant, we'll have new ideas or dreams develop over time. Unexpected opportunities and even challenges will pepper our path as well. If we're willing to keep pressing forward on the roadmap we had hoped for when we started, we'll need to be committed to evolving and getting better every single day as a student of whatever business or category we find ourselves in. Being audible-ready and systems driven are the keys to continuous success over the course of a long career, but they're also how we'll make a positive impact on the lives of others along the way.

> *Being audible-ready means never settling for status quo and continually looking for opportunities to grow, change, stretch, and share.*

— CHAPTER 5 —

Believe in Something
Bigger Than Yourself

WHEN I WAS young, in the wake of my parent's divorce, it fell to me to make sure that my mother had what she needed to manage her severe anxiety, as well as the medication she depended on to treat a serious nervous condition. I was 16 and balancing growing up with the responsibility to care for my mother that I felt so heavy on my shoulders. I found joy in caring for my mom, but there was always a shadow in the back of my mind, knowing what I wanted to provide for her, and knowing realistically what I could actually afford.

My mother's favorite place to be is by the water, and I knew that I wanted to find a house, rental, or condo that would offer her the peace and calm that she craved. I wanted a high-end living space for her and something she could settle into long term.

I wanted so much for my mother, and I wanted to be the one who supplied all of it. This wasn't just because she had done so much for me, but also because it was a dream left unfulfilled for my grandmother. All of the summers spent playing in my grandmother's yard, pacing behind her in the house while she cooked in that cramped and dingy kitchen, and evenings watching her have to traipse outside in the darkness to find running water or use the restroom, left me wanting more for her. I wanted my grandmother's living situation to improve, and I wanted to be the one to provide those improvements. Sadly, we ran out of time with her before I could make good on my promises and dreams. I did not want that for my mother.

As my bank account began to swell, I knew I wanted to move my mom into the type of home on the water she had always mentioned to me. I soon found what she was looking for and put down the rental payment so she could move in and make it her own. It wasn't my dream location or home, and as a rental it was more temporary than I was comfortable with, but it was still a beautiful spot and a safe, clean, and spacious home that would provide for her in the moment until I could find something even better.

Then the downturn hit in 2008. For 11 months, I fought the good fight, trying to keep myself and my assets afloat, but, as you know, that wasn't how it unfolded in real life. My business dissolved and almost every single dime I had was accounted for to pay off investors and my debtors. I was one day late on my mom's rent and I called the owner to let him know the situation. I begged him to please not kick my mom out; I would figure something out. He gave me 30 days' worth of grace but then, understandably, told us we had to move on.

I was stunned to be in this position. I had been at the top of my game just months earlier, earning millions each year and able to afford homes not only for myself but my mother and my son, as well as a fleet of cars and an expensive wardrobe. It was the gut punch of a lifetime. I looked at different options, asking if the owner had another property that was cheaper so I could move her into it temporarily then move her back once I got my finances in order. He said, "No." I was getting no traction. I knew, as I hung up the phone with the landlord, that I would have to do something I never dreamed would be required of me.

I walked up to my mom's rental house, the one I had promised was hers, and broke the news that she would have to move out because I couldn't afford her rent. In that moment, as a grown man sitting in front of his elderly mother, I was once again a 15-year-old kid in Las Vegas, calling her to let her know I had moved away without warning or even a hug. These two disappointments that were, in my view, some of my greatest failures, seemed so strongly connected. I had failed her once again, and it was heart-wrenching.

My mom, like many moms, believes I can do anything. In her mind, I was a multimillionaire who had limitless potential and never struggled with setbacks. Her condition prevents her from touching reality too closely, so I spared her the details of my financial situation and simply painted a picture of what the future could be. Over and over again, she would ask me how I could be in this predicament based on where I had been before. I tried my hardest to make the best of a bad moment, but it was killing me inside.

I moved my mother out of the water-front rental and into a much cheaper apartment that was within the budget I could scrape together. With every cardboard flap I taped shut, I vowed that I could do better. As I stacked moving boxes and stuffed a lifetime's worth of my mother's belongings into the back of a rented moving van, I believed that my sheer will and talent, along with God's grace, would see me through to the other side of this. Downgrading my mother's lifestyle when I promised her and wanted to give her so much more would not be the end of this story. I believed wholeheartedly that I could do better and committed that I would.

> *I believed wholeheartedly that I could do better and committed that I would.*

Of course, it took longer than I had hoped. But when I did ultimately get my feet back on the ground, I improved my mom's lifestyle as well. Providing her with security and a place to call home was a big goal in addition to getting my own house in order, but I waited and pushed and continued to believe that I could reach this lofty goal for myself and for her.

When I was finally ready and able to buy what I had always wanted for her, I didn't tell her right away. I picked her up and drove her to her new home, playing off the trip like we were going to visit a friend. When we turned into the neighborhood, she gasped, awestruck by how beautiful the home exteriors and landscaping were. We pulled into the driveway and her words started tumbling out, "This place is gorgeous! Who do you know here? Look at this house!" I pretended to be on my phone and asked her to give me a second while I went inside to see my friend. Instead, I pulled the house keys from out of my pocket to go inside and then walked out through the open garage door. I continued with my fake phone call and motioned for her to join me. As we toured through the house, she admired the luxury furnishings and finishes throughout the home—marble countertops, stainless steel appliances, hardwood floors, modern fixtures, and expansive windows—and finally she said, "Boy, this is a beautiful place. I would really love a place like this someday." I grinned, setting down my phone. "Really, Mom?" I asked her. She was still out of the loop about what was happening. As I handed her the keys to her new home—one she never dreamed could be hers and one I kept faith all along I could make happen—her eyes widened and then she collapsed into my arms in tears. She started to thank God for the place and rejoiced all through the kitchen, then the living room, and finally the backyard. It was a milestone I believed I would hit, but achieving it within the time frame I wanted was an accomplishment I was proud of.

Faith for the Hard Times

We store a lot of untapped potential in tomorrow. Tomorrow is the place we put lofty dreams that we know could be ours if we reached high enough but don't want to make the sacrifices to get there today. Tomorrow is our storage unit where we keep unrealized dreams safe and untouched. But the truth is, we don't know if tomorrow will ever come.

Tomorrow didn't come for me when it came to providing that dream for my grandmother, and I wasn't going to allow tomorrow to never arrive for my mother. I could not have lived with myself if I had not been able to do that for my mother, especially after I was unable to do so for my grandmother. There were so many factors that were not in my favor when it came to buying that beautiful luxury home for my mother, but I believed, even after everything fell apart, that I could make it happen. I knew my own potential and talent, and I knew what I was capable of. I believed in myself and I believed in my goals and dreams.

There are times when we don't have faith in ourselves, even when we have what it takes to succeed. I had a former NFL player on my sales team one time who sold Cadillacs for me with this same disastrous combination. He was a six-foot-six incredible statue of a man and an unbelievable salesman. He was by far one of the most knowledgeable team members when it came to product details that I have ever known. He had so much going for him: He was dynamic and easy to be around, and the customers loved him. But he had this odd Achilles' heel that rendered him unable to close a sale. I'd watch him from across the sales floor, his customers completely absorbed into his pitch, but when it came time to ask for a sale, he'd choke. It was like watching a giant transform into a mouse. His charisma would escalate and heighten and then spontaneously dissolve until he had zero confidence.

One day he came to my office to ask for some guidance about how to overcome his fears. There were two levels of managers between us, and I was at his store infrequently, so I didn't know much of his backstory. As I began to learn more about him, I discovered that he had two small boys that meant the world to him. I asked about the kinds of fatherly conversations he had with those two boys, and he described moments when he helped them overcome their own little boy fears. He explained how, in a loving dad voice, he would teach them how brave they were and how the fears they were succumbing to were not as real as they believed them to be.

After he was done, I showed him how to reframe the moment of a sale using that same idea. When you have a customer in front of you, I told him, I want you to hear the voices of your two boys doing the same for you and telling you not to be afraid. I helped him picture his boys pleading with him and patting him on the back saying, "I need you to believe right now, Dad, that you're doing this for us and that you can do it."

He started to use that distinct strategy on the sales floor when he approached the moment of asking for a sale. Instead of feeling insecure and self-conscious when the conversation drifted toward the point of purchase, he would picture his little boys assuring him that he could and needed to make the sale and close the deal. From my spot across the salesroom floor, I watched as his previous insecurities melted into a newly discovered confidence. With that strategy in place, he became one of our best closers. By using the same method that he taught his own boys, telling them in his loving fatherly voice that they didn't have to be afraid, he listened to the sound of his children speaking encouragement to him. When he couldn't rely on his own belief in himself, he relied on the beliefs of others.

During the banner year times and also when life seems its bleakest, I've been thankful for a faith I can fall back on. I am definitely no angel and preaching is not something I'm qualified to do, but my grandmother did a good job leading me down a path of belief that we all have a much higher purpose, that there is someone we can count on and believe in, and that what's most important in our lives is faith. The personal relationship I've been able to form with God has strongly influenced the relationships I have with the people around me. I live believing that we have to have both to thrive: a relationship with God and a relationship with others.

You might not consider yourself a "person of faith." That phrase holds different meanings and carries different implications for everyone, I know. But even if you wouldn't choose faith as something you cling to or lean on when things get rough, you are still a faithful person. Everyone has something they believe in, even if that's faith in our family bonds, the goodness of humankind, or ourselves. What we believe in shapes us, enables us, and informs our priorities. Faith provides a template for who we want to be and then helps us stay within the boundaries of what we hoped for ourselves and our family.

> *What we believe in shapes us, enables us, and informs our priorities.*

With that said, how does your faith show up in your day-to-day life? If I were your coworker, family member, or client, what tangible ways would I notice your faith being expressed? I don't mean how would you evangelize your beliefs. I mean how would that faith change you, your career, your successes, and your family stability?

For me, faith means knowing that I can keep pushing, striving, and edging closer to my goals because I have someone above who sees me and cares about my actions. It also means that I want to live with integrity, treat people well, and show an interest in the concerns of those around me. My faith makes me a better leader and an executive who considers the lifestyles and needs of the people on the every rung of the ladder, not just the ones who sit with me around the executive table.

I can't think of a time when, regardless of how grim my life might have gotten, God wasn't there to pull me through. He always made a way. I have faith that he will continue to make that happen.

You know, they say that you can't pray and worry at the same time because you have to pick one. I prefer to pray, and that's the truth. Even though it's easier said than done, I have to hold myself accountable for that practice, and remind myself that God has always made a way for me.

In my life, faith means trusting that God is with me, for me, and ahead of me on the path at all times. Of course, my hope would be that you would find peace in a relationship with God too, but I also respect that we all come from different backgrounds and hold different beliefs. Regardless of where our faith lies, at some point in our lives, storms are going to show up at our door and the winds will howl and test the foundations. Whatever we've built our lives upon will come under attack at some point, so it's imperative that we have a strong and true foundation in our friends, our circles of influence, and the faith that we believe will see us through. Because the storm is going to come. It's just a matter of when.

Finding What Wakes You Up

When the alarm starts beeping in the morning, and the sun isn't yet shining through the curtains, it can be tempting to push snooze. But when we do that, we're not just snoozing that particular day, we're also snoozing our lives one morning at a time. Instead, before the alarm even sounds, I spring out of bed with a list of to-dos rattling around my mind.

Whatever waits for me on the other side of the morning, I know God will see me through. When I get there, I have a motivation and drive that comes from the understanding that my family is dependent on what I can create, accomplish and build that day. It's my faith that gets me up and my family that keeps me up.

What wakes you up in the morning? Maybe, like me, the need to provide for your family and their futures is always on your mind. Maybe you have big goals and aspirations that you want to achieve before time slips away, or working is something you want to quit doing altogether, with an early retirement at the forefront of your thoughts. Identify what or who energizes your list of priorities, especially when those priorities and tasks begin to feel burdensome, and tap into the motivation they provide.

> It's my faith that gets me up and my family that keeps me up.

Sometimes, when we're punching a clock or slogging away at a task that feels monotonous or below our abilities, we can lose sight of the impact our efforts are making. If we're providing for our family, it's easy to remember that our efforts are benefiting them. But do we really allow ourselves to realize what our seemingly small achievements are doing? When we plug away at a 40- or 50- or 60-hour work week, that sacrifice of our time is feeding our family. When we take overtime to sock away extra money or enthusiastically greet every customer that walks through the door so we can become the top sales leader on the board and take home that month's bonus check, we can forget that these incredible efforts are paying for dance lessons for our daughters or the mortgage for an elderly parent. But zoom out a bit and take a look at the implications beyond even those immediate needs.

Those overtime hours, the extra sacrifices, and all of the predawn clock-punching moments that make your stomach turn aren't for nothing. Feeding your children and paying for their sports teams or putting them through college affects so much more than just your one child. Raising and educating a child can have a global impact. Your commitment and faithful work may benefit your child, but it also benefits us all. One more healthy, happy, educated person in the world is an incredible contribution. So, when it feels like what you're doing and what you're working toward doesn't matter, remember that by changing one life, you're changing the world. What you do matters, but who you're working for, whether that's your kids at home or a business full of employees who look to you for their weekly paycheck, your efforts are important and make an impact far greater than you could possibly know.

One more healthy, happy, educated person in the world is an incredible contribution.

Winning with Integrity

I've been in sales my entire career. From my days selling used cars from a pay-phone outside of Caesar's Palace to running multimillion-dollar operations, sales are my roots. I've learned from some of the greatest sales professionals in the industry, and I've unlocked some of the most important keys to success. Amid all of that growth and experience, the most powerful tool I've yet found is to remember what the consequences of a yes or a no from a customer will be in my life. This is so important that I want to reiterate it again: If you can get a customer to say yes, you won't have to tell your family no.

When I'm standing on the sales floor or sitting around a conference table, the needs and wants of my family are there with me, too. If I'm not successful in providing the product and services that the customer wants, to the point that they will purchase from me right then and there, then I have to go home with the knowledge that I have one more no to say to my family. I would so much rather end each day knowing I could go home with at least one yes, if not a handful or armload of them. This doesn't mean persuading a customer to buy something they aren't looking for or creating a high-pressure pitch that they finally succumb to. It's doing your due diligence and putting in the time and effort to create a positive interaction for both you *and* the customer.

You might not believe in the same God I do, but having faith in something bigger than yourself can make your life and your business better. Sometimes when we're focused on winning, we believe that reaching that trophy means winning at all costs. That frame of mind may bring you wins in the short run, but over time, the casualties to that system will be so great, as clients begin to lose trust in you or coworkers don't consider you to be a team player, that the wins won't be sustainable. That mentality creates a wasteland of burned bridges in your wake.

Winning and winning consistently requires that we hold to standards of integrity and honesty and that we recognize we are not the ultimate power in the room. Even if we're sitting at the head of the table or the top of the organizational chart, we're more effective and efficient when we remember that we answer to something bigger and more important than ourselves. Holding onto faith in God, for me, has kept me in check when my authority, bank account, or voice became so powerful that I could have recklessly improved my own life without considering the lives and needs of others. In those times of excess, it can be tempting to allow ourselves to think only of ourselves. Being reminded of how small we are in comparison to a big and all-powerful and all-knowing God sets me straight when no one else has the empowerment or access to me to do so.

Because you're spending time with me to learn these principles and you make growth a part of your life, I believe you have what it takes to be a winner. I know from experience that once someone gets into that mindset of relentlessly pursuing a win, it can be difficult to back away from a guaranteed win, even if it calls for disappointing your conscious or harming someone else's career. But I can assure you that no win is worth your reputation. Whether you win or not matters, but just as important is the way in which you win.

I've been around plenty of people who chose winning at all costs, and some of them have been very successful. But I would be lying if I didn't also mention that their wins didn't come without a price I'm not willing to pay either socially or at home. You, too, have a choice to make. If you have a belief system you ascribe to, ask yourself how it affects the way you approach work and your relationships with those around you. If the impact faith has on your work life is non-existent, then it's time to consider just how important those beliefs are to you and whether you are allowing them to make a difference in your life at all.

If you don't have a set of beliefs that you hold to, I want to encourage you to consider what priorities you could set in your life that would create boundaries around what constitutes healthy winning and protects you from a style of winning that leaves desolation in the rearview mirror and limits your options in the future. Faith may not be something you're willing to dive into for now. That's, of course, up to you and your set of family values. But, for me, faith in God has improved my scorecard in ways that aren't just about coming out on top. Believing in a power that transcends my limited abilities and short lifespan puts all of my wins, losses, and all the things I'm striving toward into perspective. Winning doesn't require faith, but holding onto faith has made me a better winner.

> **Winning doesn't require faith, but holding onto faith has made me a better winner.**

— CHAPTER 6 —

Post-Game Wrap Up

F YOU FEEL like life has benched you, I hope the time we've spent together in this book has reminded you that you're worthy of being called in for the starting lineup. I hope the fears that plague you as you stand on shaky knees and walk with trepidation toward the game field have been tempered by some helpful and practical resources, mantras, and practices that will shore you up when you feel like there's no way you can face the competition or task ahead of you.

For those of us who were benched because of a family who didn't believe in your ability or who cut you down for every mistake or fumble, it can feel like it takes everything you've got just to show up. Stepping onto the playing field is a courageous act, and I want to make sure that you know what a big deal that is. I've watched so many people bench themselves out of fear, so the fact that you're willing to be in the mix and a part of the fray is admirable. But once you step out on the field, your role in the game is just getting started. Showing up is half the battle, but there's still a game to be played.

As you step onto whatever the game field is for you—a gym, a cubicle, a sales floor—remember to visualize who you want to be, the results you want to see, and the goal you want to hit by the end of the day. Starting with the small particulars of your routine may be a helpful place to begin. Mentally go over every detail of your day: who you need to make connections with over coffee that could further your career, what extra project you could take on to catch the eye of your supervisor, what strategy you could implement to make one more sale today than you did yesterday.

> ...visualize who you want to be, the results you want to see, and the goal you want to hit by the end of the day.

As you visualize these steps, remember to always see yourself winning in whatever way or result that matches your specific career or aspirations. If you're an athlete, picture the scoreboard and see yourself catching the game-winning touchdown; if you're a salesperson, picture your sales totals at the end of the day and see your name at the top of your manager's whiteboard list; if you're an entrepreneur, visualize new clients flocking to your website or inbox eager to purchase the original new product or service only you can offer.

Starting every day with a winning mindset is crucial. I can't stress that enough. But even when we're trying our best to set a winning tone for the day, we can have a tendency to miss our own blind spots. We all have negative patterns of thinking that we're inclined to fall into but getting your head in the game means recognizing the symptoms early before a losing mindset has a chance to take over. Take notice when you start to question your own talent or feel yourself fill with dread before going to a sales meeting because of the challenges and feedback that you'll receive there. In those moments, visualizing victory is more important than ever if you're going to fight back against the negativity that our brains so readily offer when we're faced with resistance.

It's also vital to keep your homecourt advantage right there with you. I will never, for as long as I live, forget the feeling of waking up in a car after a restless night sprawled out uncomfortably across the seats and floorboards. As I stood in that boiling Arizona parking lot outside of the Ritz Carlton, gathering my thoughts and clothes as I prepared for the interview we had driven across the country for. It was 119 degrees that day and sweltering. But I wasn't alone. I know the support of someone who cared about me was the reason I was able to go to that interview and not give up on my dream.

In the midst of disheartening times, call in your home court advantage. You'll be tempted to step off the field altogether or call a timeout so that you can tuck your tail and run. Instead, ask those who are in your corner cheering for you to give you healthy feedback on what you see as failures and listen to their encouragement. Soak up what it feels like to not be in the game alone and then run back onto the field.

With that renewed energy, tap into why you're in the game in the first place. Is it to pay off the debt that weighs you down? Is it to prove to yourself and others that you're more than just a timecard that gets punched five days a week? Dig down to where your burning desire to win resides and tap into that urgency. When we understand why we're working and the goal we're striving toward, staying in the game is not only more likely but more enjoyable. Remembering why we're pushing so hard enables us to show up at a higher level.

> *Remembering why we're pushing so hard enables us to show up at a higher level.*

Plugging away for 40-plus hours a week at the same job with no room for promotion or growth is honorable if it puts food on the table for your family. But if you've got big ambitions of making more out of your career and life, being your own boss, setting your own agenda and hours, and leaving something grand behind as a legacy for your children when you leave this earth, then the monotony of doing things the way you always have is not going to cut it. As in football, quick and easy lateral passes sometimes gain you yardage, but it's the Hail Mary passes that make the highlight reel. In other words, you need both safe steps and risky leaps to succeed.

Too often in our culture we equate playing it safe with playing well. I wholeheartedly disagree. Playing it safe is meant for baby proofing the house or wearing a helmet when riding a motorcycle, but it has a limited place in the career of someone who holds big ambitions. Playing it safe doesn't mean avoiding just the opportunities or steps that are outrageous and overtly dumb. Playing it safe means avoiding *all* risks, even the ones that could catapult you into the next level of your career or success. Playing it safe means staying average, and by committing to reading this book you've already proven that you're more than that.

What some people call risk-averse, I call Chicken Little Syndrome. For those who won't allow themselves to take even cautious and calculated risks, the sky is always falling or on the verge of crumbling above their heads. People cling to Chicken Little Syndrome because they don't want to lose anything, but when they fold their arms across their chest and refuse to budge or step into any type of discomfort or uncertainty, what they have unintentionally done is lose everything, including the potential for improvement, intimacy, or the joy that can be found in the unexpected twists and turns life offers us when we are willing to try something new.

For me, and for the people I've worked with, I'm a firm believer that this fear of instability originated with one specific moment or situation. Something occurred for that mindset to form. As I'm working with leaders who struggle with this mentality, I like to almost hypnotize them in a way where I go back to that moment where they first felt like they lost at life and then help them fix that moment. I do my level best to help them fix that original memory because once we do, everything else is allowed to fall into place.

If we go back to the root of what makes us feel like failures, we can learn to change our growing patterns. With the power of knowing our drivers and how those memories or old ideas affect us, we're able to tap into that feeling and not let it consume us when it could take us down in defeat.

Viewing Losses as Lessons

Losing, no matter how great the loss, is not a life sentence. As someone who has lost many times before—and lost *big*—I want to encourage you to understand that losses are just lessons in disguise. When things don't go our way and we just chalk up one more failure, we don't allow ourselves the opportunity and ability to improve ourselves and our chances to win the next time that occasion arises again. But when we view losses as lessons, the experience becomes a positive one that teaches us how to move forward with gusto and confidence, having tucked one more valuable tool into our toolbox that will make the next opportunity that much more viable and our likelihood of winning that much greater.

The difference between a loser and a leader is the willingness to accept and enact change even when it's frightening and especially when it's not popular. Customers, clients, and coworkers will always resist change because change is not comfortable. But to stay at the forefront of the pack, leaders have to be willing to be comfortable with discomfort. Leaders like Blockbuster and Toys R Us evolved over time into losers because they weren't willing to look up from their winning scoresheet to see the challenges and threats that loomed on the horizon ahead of them. If they had been eager to tweak their systems and admit that just because they won in the past didn't mean they would win forever, these mega corporations might still be the gold standard for innovation and entertainment instead of examples of stubborn and prideful Goliaths who were taken down by opponents they didn't believe to be threats.

> *The difference between a loser and a leader is the willingness to accept and enact change even when it's frightening and especially when it's not popular.*

As you prepare for the future in your specific industry, take notes from the colleagues who are being promoted faster than you or the competing companies who are scooping up your market share. It's possible they understand something you haven't picked up on yet or are capitalizing on a market trend that hasn't yet crossed your desk. Instead of wallowing in the loss of customers or lamenting the lack of zeroes on the end of your paycheck, ask yourself how you can take the new methods and unique approaches used by those who are beating you and tweak them to your advantage. Even if you think the market is stable, your career is set and the customers you've targeted will always be predictable, be unabashedly willing and ready like Manning to yell "Omaha" whenever you see a new and unexpected opening on the field that could take you where you want to go in your career faster.

Remember Your Reasons

I hope during our time together you've been able to identify what triggers your desire to get out of bed every morning. For me, it's my faith in God and a passion to provide as much as I possibly can for all the members of my family, while leaving the community where I live in a better place. Even if you don't consider yourself a faith-filled person, the things you believe to be true in your life will be the things that motivate you to spring out of bed, woken by the faith that fuels you and the people that drive you.

I've shared these principles with you because I want you to bring the talents that are specific to you and your experience out into the world. I've passed them on to you with confidence that they can make a difference because they have radically changed my life and the trajectory of my career over time. Even when my career resided at the bottom of the barrel, when I was sleeping in my girlfriend's car and relying on the kindness of others for shelter and food, it was these principles and a relentless spirit that propelled me back to where I was before the bottom fell out of the economy, and then even further.

Using those principles, I took another big step on the rung of my career. With my experience running multiple dealerships and working in every department that a car dealership has to offer, I recently had the opportunity to assume the role of President and Chief Executive Officer for a luxury dealership in Northern Virginia. The former CEO was Thomas Moorehead, also a former chairman of the National Association for Minority Dealers (NAMAD). Moorehead made waves by being the first African American Rolls Royce dealer, the first African American Lamborghini dealer, and the first African American McLaren dealer. He was one of only five minority BMW dealers and one of only two Mini Cooper dealers.

At the age of 75, with all of these accomplishments, as well as 48 hotels in his possession, he was ready to enjoy the fruits of his labor and spend more time in his Miami home. To do so, he needed someone with a vision for expansion, who could list both experience with big platform and a corporate background on his or her resume. He was looking for someone to take his business to the next level. During my time as the leader of his operation, I'm honored to say that I did that. Sales improved month over month, and during my leadership tenure, the dealership experienced its most profitable time in its 20-year history.

This move to overseeing a company that is nearly three-quarters of a billion dollars deep in revenue was obviously a huge win, but my core principles have taught me that there was no room for complacency. This is the time for me to evolve and get better every day as a student of my specific craft, industry, and business. If I'm going to make an impact on my career and the lives of my family members, I knew I had to focus on getting better and growing even when everything was going well.

So I have taken the biggest step in my career to date and started Paul White Enterprises, an organization dedicated to improving the lives of sales teams and communities beyond my immediate sphere. Standing at the pinnacle of my career, I can see the valleys I had to cross to get where I am today. While others may only see the highlight reel of my *after* and not the pain of my *before*, I know better. I can see the deep and wide canyon that was my life in the aftermath of the 2008 economic downturn. I can see the discouraging deserts filled with empty promises made by managers and leaders who promised they would help accelerate my career and then exited their specific roles or companies before they could make good on their word. These types of setbacks happened even when I was in admirable and prestigious positions. The higher I've climbed in my career, the more obvious it has become to me how important humility is to stay relevant and helpful.

Now, as I embark on this exciting journey toward leading in a new way through my own company, I'm even more grateful for the lessons and leadership I encountered along my journey. I pray I can continue this legacy long into the future no matter what road I choose to travel.

My Challenge to You

Now that you have these powerful resources and principles at your disposal, I have every expectation that your career path will reach new heights as well. As you enjoy those, I want to challenge you to focus on cultivating a humble servant attitude.

The best way to maintain a focus on humility, serving others, and remaining teachable is to surround yourself with other people who share your approach. That doesn't mean they don't dress the part—I love clothes more than the average person. It means they're willing to help others selflessly even when they have to put themselves and their own advantages second.

> *I want to challenge you to focus on cultivating a humble servant attitude.*

This kind of service is important for my mental health, I've found, as it keeps me from thinking more highly of myself than I should, but it also prevents people from being threatened by any success I may achieve. When you sit at the head table and lead the room, there is always a potential for people to see your wins as a personal attack on their own careers. When you put them first, even if that means putting in extra time to help them succeed, the work atmosphere around you shifts for the better.

Culture won't always line up with this way of working or thinking. It's an approach that may seem unnatural to you, and it may appear odd to your coworkers at first. But part of being a strong leader is knowing who you are and who you are not. It means not cutting corners at the expense of the people you're leading so that you can get ahead, and it means making the tough choices even when they're not popular to keep the ship pointed in the right direction. Becoming the best version of yourself as a leader, and as an individual, is an ever-evolving process.

Business in general is the same in that it never stays the same. When it comes to the work world, there are only two options: Either it gets better, or it gets worse. When we're honest, we realize that that describes us, too. We can look down on mega corporations who don't see change coming, but if we're not feeding ourselves, then we're in a similar process of decaying in our careers. When we're not sharpening our saw and becoming better at what we do and better versions of ourselves, then we're on a slow downward slope, sliding further and further from the pinnacle of our goals.

Maintaining this focus on humility and accepting the challenge to stay teachable is another reason I stress the importance of a daily checkout system. If you know the score from yesterday, then you can learn to improve the score today. If you're constantly running an inventory on yourself and your abilities, then when you wake up in the morning, you know exactly where to spend time and where your biggest area of opportunity lies. That's how I live, and I hope, after our time together, it's how you'll choose to live as well.

Even if you try your hardest, I know there will be times when, in spite your best efforts, you don't win. Those are the moments that haunt us. It's the moments like my boardroom presentation when I gave it everything I had to win the dealership opening in Texas. I was in the top three. I had a verbal confirmation from one of the hiring executives that I was a shoe-in. And then I wasn't. It was a crushing moment that could have defined my career or marked the ending for me. I had failed so many times before that moment that I could have simply decided my luck had run out, I didn't have what it took anymore, or any other number of lies that I could have believed in order to move past the pain of losing when I had done everything I could to win. Of course, as you know, that's not my story's ending.

When you don't get immediate results from your efforts in leadership or in life, it can be easy to believe the system is broken, the tools don't work, and you weren't meant to reside in the winner's circle. Those moments can be career killers because they're extremely powerful. The emotion that waits behind rejection is brutal, and it reminds us of all of our past failures, as well as our current ones. When those moments arise, and you need an extra push, remember how my multimillion-dollar successes are punctuated by a long stretch of time when I had nothing, couldn't legally drive and slept in the trunk of a car in a parking lot. Wherever you're at may not be anywhere near the rock bottom where I lived for an uncomfortably long period of time. But if you are at rock bottom, let me encourage you as someone who has been there, that the best way to get out is to start climbing and clawing your way back to the top right now.

If the negativity begins to drown out the positive, sit down, grab a pen, and write out as many wins in your past as you can recall. There are more than you realize, I can assure you. Did you get an education? Write it down. How about a successful marriage or friendship, kids who are well-fed and loved, or a house that has running water? Did you get out of bed this morning? Those accomplishments are all much bigger wins than you likely give yourself credit for. When we remember how we have won in the past, it can be easier to win in the future. Allow yourself the space and room to believe that you could be a winner, then look down at your lengthy list of past wins and know that it's true.

I wish I could go back in time and talk to myself during my early glory years. I wish I could look myself in the face as I passed out huge bonus checks to my team and drove around in luxury vehicles, before it all came to a crashing halt. I don't believe I was resting on my laurels at the time. I don't look back and think how foolish I was to be complacent. To the contrary, I was then, as I am now, always seeking to grow and change in spontaneous and new ways that I have never tried before. Even still, I wonder if there was something I could have done to better prepare myself for the inevitable downfall that neither I nor anyone else in the industry could have seen coming. Was there a way to stave off the fall from grace and financial collapse that nearly suffocated me during that time? Perhaps. But the memories of those hard times are a powerful reminder to me that nothing is ever certain in business.

No paycheck or promotion or investment can ever be fully trusted to be permanent. I want to implore you to remember that no success is forever, just like losing isn't a life sentence. When the wins come, and I assure you they will, remind yourself how temporary they can be. Instill a sense of urgency in yourself and the teams you lead to recognize wins as a signal to press in harder and look for weaknesses more diligently than ever. Resting after a win is like lying down in front of the finish line with a few yards to go. Stand up and keep running, being sure to high-five the competitors and teammates running alongside you. A sore winner is far more intolerable than a sore loser, so be sure to acknowledge the efforts of others and keep a sober disposition that allows you to recognize that you couldn't have gotten to where you are today without the help and commitment of others as well. Don't give up or get cocky just because you're ahead of the pack. A win signals momentum; it does not signal the finale.

Learn from My Mistakes—And Create a Winning Record

When I look back over the course of my career, I see my beginning, an unbelievably rocky start, with a difficult childhood and a biracial label to overcome. There were times when I didn't know how I would defeat the next hurdle. I just believed that I would. I dreamed up a life for myself that I hadn't really seen in my small and impoverished reality, and I persevered and struggled until I watched them became real.

There were moments along my journey, as I'm sure there have been along your own, when my dogged pursuit of success made me have a limited focus. I can look back and see that a relentlessness of that level can bring success and quickly, but it can also sow discord at home. Keeping your eyes on the horizon and being in tune with the movements, positions, and feelings of the teammates around you—whether those are actual employees or family members and friends—makes you a better leader. That way, when the alarm clock beeps loudly in the morning, you'll be able to hop out of bed excited about the day and happy with the reflection you see in the mirror, knowing who you're working for and why your work matters.

...when we wake up to win, we have to have a plan and a playbook for the game we're about to enter.

I wrote this book for you. I wrote it because I know that nobody wakes up hoping to lose, and yet, so many of us repeat the same actions that lead us to lose, day after day, year after year—sometimes for a lifetime. I know from experience that when we wake up to win, we have to have a plan and a playbook for the game we're about to enter. I wrote this book to be a roadmap for you, so you can take the principles that have worked so intensely for me over the course of my multimillion-dollar career and put them into action in whatever career you've chosen.

But more than my wins, I want you to learn from my mistakes. There are so many lessons I have learned through failure that you don't have to repeat on your own. I've already taken those routes, and I'm here today to help you stay off the roads that turn out to be dead ends. I've test driven most of them, and this book has been my way of helping you find the best roads, the fastest routes, and the safest detours. Go back, review it, reflect, and remember that you have a resource for your down times.

I truly believe everyone has a higher purpose. You have a unique greatness that this world needs. You have a niche specialty and an uncommon perspective that only you possess. We need you to find your why, to discover where you find your passion and your purpose best lived out, and then to pursue it with relentless drive and hunger.

My exact lessons, opportunities, strengths, and weaknesses that I've shared with you in these pages may not fit perfectly when you duplicate them in your own life. You may not be the executive leader of multiple luxury car dealerships or the owner of your own business. But even if you are, your unique life and viewpoint will require you to tailor and customize these principles to your own career and interests. I hope, in spite of our differences, that you've found common ground in my purpose with these pages, and these lessons will serve as a solid jumping off point for you as you charge out of bed tomorrow, ready to step up and create a winning record.

Like I mentioned earlier in our time together, I like to surround myself with Game Changers and Playmakers. Your interest in this topic alone tells me so much about your drive and spirit, and I want to add you to my circle of influence. To make it easy for us to connect, please visit paulwhiteent.com and introduce yourself. There are so many more resources and ideas not in the limited pages of this book that I'd like to share with this enthusiastic community of readers and leaders as we make connections in the coming months. I look forward to learning from you and your experiences as well.

I can't end our time together without reminding you that you have what it takes to be a winner. There is no *before* that disqualifies you from the *after* you deserve. Anyone can develop the confidence, training, and skills to succeed in their field, and that includes you. Don't eliminate yourself from the winner's circle before you even take the chance of stepping on the field. You've tried that before, and plugging away at the same negative, losing routine that you've always used will never transplant you onto the winning team.

You have everything you need to win, and I'm pulling for you in my corner of the world. Now, go be the winner you were created to be.

REFERENCES

Chapter Two

https://www.nytimes.com/2014/02/23/sports/olympics/olympians-use-imagery-as-mental-training.html

https://www.inc.com/jessica-rovello/five-steps-to-visualize-success-like-an-olympian.html

https://www.newsday.com/sports/olympics/team-usa-most-olympic-medals-1.3657142

http://www.oprah.com/oprahs-lifeclass/what-oprah-learned-from-jim-carrey-video

https://www.nbcsports.com/boston/patriots/tom-bradys-overtime-record-had-patriots-confident-against-chiefs

https://www.si.com/nfl/2019/02/03/tom-brady-super-bowl-mvp-history-how-many-winner

Chapter Five

https://www.cnn.com/2018/07/13/us/last-blockbuster-america-trnd/index.html

https://www.businessinsider.com/heres-how-amazon-may-have-led-toys-r-us-demise-2017-9

https://www.businessinsider.com/why-toys-r-us-is-closing-stores-2018-3

https://www.businessinsider.com/amazon-walmart-target-killed-toys-r-us-2018-3

CPSIA information can be obtained
at www.ICGtesting.com
Printed in the USA
BVHW011057200621
609988BV00012B/568/J

Ironically, Target had a similar experience, but when they prematurely ended their contract with Amazon, they invested $2.5 billion per year to enhance their online site. Toys R Us, on the other hand, who was extremely overdue in creating their online presence, dedicated only $100 million over a three-year span to revamping their website. The company would go on to die a slow death over the next decade, but it never overcame the early missteps that happened while it was still enjoying the popularity and profit of its heyday.